CONFESSIONS OF A CARP FISHER

'The wonder of the world, the beauty and the power, the
shapes of things, their colours, lights and shades; these I
saw. Look ye also while life lasts.'

A corner of a Carp Pool.

CONFESSIONS

OF A

CARP FISHER

'BB'

Illustrated by
DENYS WATKINS-PITCHFORD
F.R.S.A., A.R.C.A.

Foreword by
FRED J. TAYLOR

White Lion Books
CAMBRIDGE

White Lion Books
an imprint of
COLT BOOKS LTD
9 Clarendon Road
Cambridge CB2 2BH
tel: (01223) 357047 fax: (01223) 365866

This edition first published by
White Lion Books 1997

ISBN 1 874762 31 7

British Library Cataloguing in Publication Data
A catalogue record for this book is available from the
British Library

Printed and bound in Great Britain by
Biddles Ltd, Guildford and King's Lynn

TO
RICHARD WALKER

ACKNOWLEDGEMENTS

The extract from *Coarse Fishing* by Hugh Sheringham is reproduced by permission of Messrs. A. & C. Black, Ltd., and the contributions by Flt.-Lt. Burton, Richard Walker, Esq., Albert Buckley, Esq. and L. D. Davis, Esq. by permission of the authors concerned.

CONTENTS

FOREWORD

"I am looking forward to reading 'BB's *Confessions of a Carp Fisher*," wrote Maurice Ingham in one of his many early letters to Richard Walker. This exchange of letters, over a period of several years, was later published in its entirety under the title *Drop Me a Line*. In the book both authors referred to the imminent publication of *Confessions* with a great deal of enthusiasm.

In fact, the first edition appeared in 1950 and, like all 'BB's other works, it was considered to be a classic. It is somewhat sobering to think that almost half a century has passed since then! I could not begin to count the number of times I have read it. My first edition was borrowed and never returned. My second edition is dog-eared and tatty, and I refuse to lend it to anyone!

That is why this new edition is so special. Carp fishing has become a cult rather than a sport and *Confessions of a Carp Fisher* has long been an important part of the development of carp fishing. It will tell the modern angler little about techniques or tactics but it portrays a deep understanding of the fish themselves. You do not have to be a carp fisher, or indeed even a fisher, to become deeply engrossed in the mysteries that surround these fish.

'BB' is adamant that his book is not about tackle but about the fish itself. It is for "those who know the hush of a summer night when every bush and tree takes on a watchful shadow". You do not have to be a carp devotee to appreciate those comments but, if you *are*, you will agree that there is indeed more to fishing than catching fish. 'BB' always knew that.

At no point in the book does 'BB' suggest any expertise on his part. In fact, he goes to some lengths to advise the reader of his own inadequacy. He forecast, in my earlier edition, that bigger carp than Walker's 44-pounder would be caught. "One day," he wrote, "we may hear of a 50-pounder. It may be caught by Walker himself or by an angler of similar calibre." He then adds, "certainly not by me, whose wandering eye strays too often from his tackle." We, who have been the same route many times, are no less guilty ourselves. 'BB' not only understood carp; he understood carp anglers too, and it is fitting that he should have lived long enough to see his prediction come true when Chris Yates took his 50+-pounder from Redmire pool. Chris, along with many other modern young carp anglers, became close friends with 'BB' who is to this day regarded as the Father Figure of the sport.

We spoke on the telephone and we exchanged letters. We quoted each other in our numerous articles for the press but, alas, our paths never crossed. Today I regard that fact as a bad mistake on my part. I was active when 'BB' was not. I should have joined my many young friends and made the same effort as they did. It was my fault and it will always be my great loss.

This new edition of *Confessions of a Carp Fisher* will help to satisfy the desires of younger carp historians. Make no mistake about it, carp history has been recorded and will go on being recorded alongside that of the lordly salmon. 'BB' played a bigger part than most in its documenting because he was always aware of the basics. You cannot move on to greater things until you have absorbed the basics. That is what 'BB's confessions (if such they were) offer to the already well-equipped and highly-technical expert. He knew all about the 'atmosphere' of the most demanding of all fish and, while he took pleasure in defeating his quarry from time to time, his greatest joy came from pitting his wits and unlimited patience against his unseen and silent adversary. The need for concealment and stealth are somewhat invalidated by the extreme distance-casting tackle used today by modern carp anglers, but the fundamentals remain unaltered. If you apply stealth and low cunning, you will have one more advantage over whatever fish you seek to catch.

And if you appreciate the dark hours when "the mist wreathes across the black mirror of the pool and only the owls, rats and foxes are awake", you are more than half-way towards being a sucessful carp angler. You will be on par with the late 'BB' himself, and you can surely feel proud to be so!

FRED J. TAYLOR
1997

Chapter I

THE CHARACTER OF THE
CARP FISHER

I CAN do no better, at the very beginning of the first chapter, than to quote a passage from Mr. Ransome's delightful collection of fishing essays *Rod and Line*, Jonathan Cape Ltd., which passage first put into my mind this little book.

'A true record of the life of an habitual carp fisher would be a book to set beside De Quincey's *Confessions of an Opium Eater,* a book of taut nerves, of hallucinations, of a hypnotic state (it is possible to stare a float into invisibility), of visions, Japanese in character of great blunt-headed, golden fish, in golden spray, curving in the air under sprays of weeping willow, and then rare moments when this long-drawn-out tautness of expectation is resolved into a frenzy of action.'

This then is what I am setting out to do, to record my own experiences with these fish and to include the experiences of other people, who have brought to bank and safely 'cased' specimen carp.

First, however, you must know that among fishermen there are many divers kinds and they fall into definite classes. The well-to-do are 'game' fishers, angling for salmon and trout; rarely does the rich man think that 'coarse' fish are worth his notice. He is a man who needs movement and change, his tastes are expensive, so is his tackel. He will not read this book.

Salmon and trout are the rich man's sport; the poor man must be content with coarse fish. Among coarse fishers also there are many types. There is the man who, if he were rich and in a different station of life, would be a fly fisher, a man who must have constant action, and, if possible, plenty of sport. He does not try for the 'big stuff', he goes 'all out' for the roach, perch, and bream—fish which will, as a general rule, always provide a full keep net or basket. He does not catch fish to eat or to preserve as specimens. The roach fisher—the successful roach fisher—is not to be sneered at. He is an artist. His tackel is fine, his 'strike' is delicate and true, as swift and polished as the action of the fly fisher, he casts beautifully with unerring aim. By the end of the day his keep net is full to overflowing—usually with dead or dying fish which might just as well be set free. But he is an artist all the same—your skilled roach fisher. Then the perch fisher—he too needs plenty of action and good bold bites—there is always something of the schoolboy about your blue-blooded perch fisher. The bite of the perch makes glad the heart of a boy—it is a determined, rather leisurely bite. Unlike the roach expert, the perch fisher will sometimes take his catch home and eat them and very good they are (so are roach for that matter, if you know how to cook them).

Then we have the pike fishers, a breezy, hardy, red-faced race of men, impervious to the wildest winter

2

weather, fond of the ale house and jolly company. They too will eat what they catch. Pike fishers, successful pike fishers, are hearty rascals, full of exciting stories of battles with fabulous monsters. Yet there are two types of pike fishers, those who spin and those who live bait. (The spinners would be fly fishers if they had the chance.) The 'live baiter' is, perhaps, the hardiest of all the tribe of Isaak. He fishes throughout the most bitter winter day, sitting on his basket, or standing with upturned coat collar, a trembling drop at the end of his nose, his red rimmed eyes (blinded with tears from the icy wind) fixed upon the dancing scarlet buoy of his 'Fishing Gazette' pike float as it bobs up and down on the leaden ripples. I take my hat off to the 'live baiter' because he has something in his make up of the habitual carp fisher, for he possesses inexhaustible patience.

There are barbel fishers (I know few barbel fishers so cannot speak with authority upon them) and there are habitual bream fishers. The latter I am told are rather coarse fellows who like to catch their fish by the stone; I suspect there is something of the fishmonger and poulterer about bream fishers. The bream is hardly an edible fish and bream fishers never—as far as I can discover—eat what they catch and small blame to them for I have tasted bream—they are almost as tasteless as chub and nearly as bony. Bream fishers are usually big, flat-footed men, retired constables and railwaymen and sometimes barbers by profession, men of little imagination. They are not so hardy as your true pike fisher. I believe there are some who fish for nothing but gudgeon. (Gudgeon scratching used to be a popular pastime on the Thames when anglers wore blazers and straw hats.) All are river men and rather nice, peaceable fellows, fond of summer evenings and camp

3

sheathings, willows and weedy scented weirs, and a tall glass of ale at the day's end. They (the gudgeon scratchers) are, I think, a partly vanished race.

And there are carp fishers, or I should say, carp addicts. These are very strange men indeed (the author is one of them). Carp fishing is a most curious form of fishing and calls for a very special turn of mind and character. First there is the quality of patience. Your habitual carp fisher is a man of inexhaustible patience, no angler born has more than he, not even a wild sad-eyed heron has greater patience and, I may add, watchfulness. He is a man of summer for the carp is a summer fish. Carp fishers disappear in autumn and are not seen until the following midsummer, nobody quite knows where they go or what they do. In my case, as soon as the summer ends, the mania leaves me, and I devote myself to other tasks and hobbies. The winter is a period of rest and recuperation for you must know there is no form of fishing which calls for greater quietness and concentration.

Most carp fishers I have met are big 'still' men, slow of movement, soft-footed and low-voiced, many have nagging lean wives (I hasten to add that I am not so afflicted) and it is by the calm secluded waters that they have found peace and quietness for their troubled lives.

Carp fishing entails long periods of inaction, when no ripple disturbs the placid pool, when the light has drained from the sky, and the trees (there are always trees about a good carp water) have grown black against the soft twilit west. Then, maybe, there is a brief period of intense action, to be succeeded again by yet longer spells of inaction and silence. Early morning and late evening will find your carp addict abroad—during the midday hours he is not visible, having left the waterside. So then after a long

4

apprenticeship, he takes upon himself something of the character of the carp—he is most active at sunrise and sunset, and the midday hour knows him not—that time when the cattle seek the shade and stand whisking their tails in the shallows, ears and eyes alert for the dreaded hum of the gadfly which will cause panic in their ruminating ranks.

In actual fact there is only one month in the whole year when you may expect to catch a really large carp, and that month is July. Nearly all the record carp have been taken in that month. It is a little difficult to understand why this is so. Whether it is that the fish are more unwary after ten months' respite, I do not know but I shrewdly suspect that such is the case.

Before we proceed further it is now necessary to describe the history and the habits of the fish in question, after which we may get down to the business of how he may be caught and of the author's (and others') personal experiences in this most difficult form of angling.

Chapter II

SOMETHING ABOUT THE CREATURE (THE CARP)

THE date of the introduction of the carp (a native of Asia) to Britain is not known. It is first mentioned in 1496 but it may have been introduced considerably earlier. It seems to attain much greater size on the continent than here but this is due, principally, I believe, to extensive culture. Carp of 30 lbs. and over are found in France and Germany but the fish found in Florida Lake near Johannesburg attain enormous weights, in the region of 50 lbs. A very big fish of 31 lbs. was taken in 1945 from the lake of Vêlodrome near Albert but carp of similar weight and over have been found dead in Mapperly Lake near Nottingham. This lake is the premier carping water in Britain to-day but they are apparently preserved and 'outsiders' cannot obtain permission to fish for them. Later in this book will be found Mr. Albert Buckley's account of catching the record carp for Britain, which account appeared in the author's *Fisherman's Bedside Book*, published by Eyre & Spottiswoode and reprinted by their kind permission.

I do not believe that the common carp ever attain such a size (26 lbs.); all those from Mapperly appear to be mirror carp, a variety of the common carp which are almost devoid of scales. They have a few scales—very large ones, here and there upon their flanks and are far from attractive fish.

The common or 'old English' carp are beautiful creatures—a rich golden bronze in colour, and fully scaled. If, however, size is the object—I am speaking now of stocking a carp water—I should strongly advise introducing mirror carp. Fish culturists will frequently sell (to the unwary) Crucian carp for stocking purposes. These never attain great size—the record to date is 4 lbs. 11 ozs. (from Broadwater Lake, Godalming) and was captured on the 25th September 1938, by a Mr. Hinson.

Crucian are beautiful fish, of a deeper, less greenish bronze than the common carp and their pectoral fins are reddish in hue. It is altogether broader and more 'breamy' in appearance.

Carp spawn in May and June and are prolific breeders —two or more male fish attend a single female. The eggs hatch in ten or fourteen days. At this period the males develop tubercles on the head, the purpose of which is obscure. Some hold the theory that they assist the male fish to grip the female but this seems to be a far-fetched theory. They are usually active at this time, frequently leaping out of the water. But this is not always the case. A carp water which is described at length later contains fish, some of great age and size, which never exhibit this habit, only on two occasions have I seen a carp jump in that pool. Usually in a weed-grown carp water the fish may be heard sucking at the weeds—especially the under side of lily pads. If a lily leaf is examined on its underside it will be seen to be covered with small semi-transparent worms and it is on these creatures the carp feed. Yet strangely enough I know of some carp waters, abounding in lilies and good fish, where this sucking sound is never heard and I can give no explanation why this is so. It is another of those mysteries which surround the carp.

Anyone wishing to breed carp must pay close attention to the following facts. The water should be deep and plentifully supplied with lilies. It should also have some shallower parts where the fish can bask and breed, for no fish other than the chub delights so much in basking in the summer heat. It should contain no other species of predatory habit such as pike or perch—roach and rudd do not matter but carp do better if they are entirely by themselves.

If you wish to obtain specimen fish they should be fed frequently during the summer with grain and bread crusts. Artificial feeding increases their size with great rapidity.

To give an instance of this. In a lake at Dallington near Northampton some common carp were introduced in 1937. The largest weighed 1½ lbs. In 1945, choosing a hot day when the fish were basking, I put out in a boat, and, gliding quietly along among the weeds, I saw fish which weighed anything from 10 lbs. to 18 lbs. One fish of 17 lbs. was caught on floating bread a week or so prior to my visit. This shows the carp must have gained as much as 2 lbs. per year, an amazing rate of growth. The Secretary of the Club informs me that for a year or two after they were introduced he fed them with grain. It is a small but very deep lake and is fished by the floating bread method described at length later in this book. These fish were ob-

8

tained from a dealer near Virginia Water. His name and address were given to me but I have most unfortunately mislaid it.[1]

No other fresh water fish in Britain is so powerful as the carp—the salmon excepted, yet even a salmon does not possess the dogged strength of a large carp. Their sagacity and wariness is a byword and very few men have captured really monster carp. The very largest have never been caught on rod and line, they have been found floating dead, having reached the natural span of years. Croxby Pond in Lincolnshire has the reputation of holding some very big fish. Mr. Otto Overbeck, a king among carp fishers, had one of 17 lbs. from this water in 1902. With the exception of Mr. Albert Buckley, Overbeck holds the record for the capture of very big carp. I have been unable to ascertain whether he is still with us but should he chance to see this book, I should be most interested to contact him. He must have had a fund of wonderful stories of his battles with big carp. Chingford Lake in Essex has some splendid fish to its credit, one of 21 lbs. 10 ozs. was captured there by Mr. A. E. Wyatt in 1926. Cheshunt, where Mr. Sheringham caught his fifteen pounder was, at one time, the premier carp water in Britain. A fish of 20 lbs. 3 ozs. was caught there by Mr. J. Andrews in October 1916—a most unusual month in which to catch a notable carp. Nineteen and eighteen pounders are too numerous to mention but the records of the capture of fish of this weight are not often available.

Compared to salmon fishing, carp fishing is far and away the more difficult art. Because of the wiliness of the fish and the lifetime's endeavour necessary to secure a

[1] The Hazelmere Trout Farm.

9

specimen worthy of a glass case, carp fishing is not followed with any enthusiasm. That is why your habitual carp fisher is a rarity. There are, however, up and down the country, private lakes and pools on big estates where truly enormous carp are found—some pools have never been fished. About two years ago, while angling for tench one still summer's eveing, I met a young Air Force officer and his wife who told me of a pool near Grantham which held giant specimens. His wife had caught an eighteen pounder without any difficulty and he had had several fish over 10 lbs. It was a private lake where the carp had been artificially fed and all fish had to be returned, but he told me that they were voracious feeders and had none of the usual cunning which is associated with the species. This was no doubt due to artificial feeding and to the fact that nobody had tried to catch them. All were captured by the floating bread method. And this brings me to the subject of how to fish for carp which must be dealt with in the following chapter.

One word as to the age of carp. This is a very uncertain point—experts disagreeing. In 1946 I sent the scale from a 4 lb. fish I caught in a Devon locality to the *Field* expert for his inspection. I wished to know the age of the fish. He replied that it is difficult to give the age of a coarse fish as it feeds more or less all the year round, unlike the salmon which feeds only in the sea and does all its growing there.

But he told me my carp was probably eight or nine years old and was in excellent condition. I could certainly believe the latter statement as the fish fought like a sea trout and took me ten minutes to bring to the net.

A few years ago, a man fishing in Harlestone Lake, on Lord Spencer's estate, nearly fell into the water when a creature like a midget submarine glided by his float. Nobody believed him when he said it was the biggest carp ever. But a year or so later another man found upon the bank a bulky carcase of unbelievable size half eaten by an otter or some other animal of the night. He took one of the scales which was as big as a five shilling piece.

Chapter III

FISHING TECHNIQUE

THE common carp, when 'in the pink' (or, as I should prefer it, 'the gold'), puzzles some unobservant people why it should be such a powerful fighter. To understand the reason, you should watch big carp on a hot day in summer when they are lying on the surface. If possible, you should be on some eminence above the water where you can look down upon them. There they lie, always in the exact centre of the pool, well out of harm's way, listlessly lolling sideways as they expose their motionless flanks to the rays of the warming sun. You will notice one thing immediately. The fish (I am speaking of the big ones) are very thick through the shoulders; the body (observed from behind and above) is seen to taper off in a fine 'stream-line', more accentuated in the carp perhaps than in any other British fish. Here lies much of the secret; the rest lies in his very large pectoral fins. These, when the fish is 'lolling', are set an an angle of about 45° to the body. When the fish is resting on the bottom of the pond, these fins act as props. It is these powerful driving 'screws', combined with the broad shoulders and the tapered body, which enable him to drive through the water at a speed which I estimate to be in the region of 40 miles an hour and I am giving a low estimate. Remember, I have been a habitual carp fisher for thirty years so I speak from experience.[1] A tench will sometimes display a considerable 'first run' when hooked, precisely for the same reason, for that species has powerful spoon-like pectoral fins but not the stream-lined body. Tench, by the way, are very similar to carp in their habits and are sometimes as wily though, when they are on the feed, you may catch large quantities of handsome fish.

But to return to the carp. His eye is small and full of porcine cunning. The tail, unlike that of the tench which is bold and broad, is forked. Carp, like other fish, vary in colour according to their environment. I have seen golden-bronze common carp, and dark greeny-bronze specimens, and yet others almost a smoky-black. In my favourite carping pool in Devon, about which I shall have much more to say later on, they are all the latter variety, though I must admit they appear more 'smoky' when in the water than when they are on the bank. These particular fish are fighting fit and as bright and perfect as a 'newly minted' dace, fresh from a clear stream. Like all fish, carp are darker on the back and pale on the belly. The fins and tails are slightly tinged with bronzey-red in some specimens, but have not the rufus hue of the Crucian. The mirror carp is always of the smoky variety—some are quite slatey-grey in tone.

[1] A friend, who fishes a water where very big 'mirrors' abound, once checked the speed of a hooked carp in its first rush. The method employed was to tie small markers or white silk at given distances up the line, and the timing was done by stopwatch.

You may attempt to catch carp in three ways. (I would ask the reader to bear in mind I am only speaking of big carp.) You may ledger for them, usually by far the deadliest method—and you may try to outwit them by floating bread crusts and you may fish for them in mid-water. Any book on coarse fishing will give details of ledgering for carp and it is a straightforward business. Personally, I use no cast whatever. I find that, in most carp water, there are weeds and snags—fallen trees and branches—and, when hooked, your fish will dash straight for these. If you are using a fine gut cast (no self-respecting carp of any size will ever be captured on gut stouter than 3x in clear water) they will invariably break you. You will have had the satisfaction of knowing what the first run of a big carp is like but that is all. The usual tackle recommended by anglers who have not specialized in carp fishing is a 2x cast, dyed to harmonise with the pond bed—a ten or twelve foot rod and a $3\frac{1}{2}$ inch Sheffield reel. Some recommend a No. 8 hook. Albert Buckley caught his twenty-six pounder on roach tackle. But then it must be remembered he had open deep water in which to wage his battle and there were few obstructions. Nevertheless his was a great achievement, only those who have played and lost big carp can know just how notable it was.

If you have a clear open water without obstructions, then I would say, by all means, fish as fine as you can, use roach tackle as Buckley did, but I know of no carp water other than Mapperly where such ideal conditions obtain.

Your average big carp water is large, surrounded or partially surrounded by trees. Old mine shafts and flooded workings are frequently inhabited by carp and trees usually grow round such places after a lapse of time. Again, as the years pass, the trees decay and fall into the pool and, once this happens, the giants are secure against anything the angler can do short of netting and draining the place. A big fish, in his first rush, will take out 100 yards of line. No other coarse fish will do this, save perhaps a barbel which is a very powerful fighter, almost as powerful perhaps as a carp.

So your reel must be a large one. I use a Milward sea reel made of bakelite. This reel, which is fitted with a check and can be used as a spinning reel, holds 200 yards of tapered line. It pays to use good line—the very best quality, with a 9 lb. breaking strain. I am wholly in agreement with those writers who advocate a strong rod—I use

Eyed Hook   Alasticum Wire

Pulled tight, spare end
wrapped round main trace

a Wallis Wizard rod—a doughty weapon specially made for me by Allcocks of Redditch. Most important of all, I never use a gut cast. Up to 1946 I always did so and lost every big fish I hooked, due to 'snaggy' water, save once, in the case of a 20 lb. fish which I lost through a piece of sheer absent-mindedness as will be described later. And then a friend suggested alasticum wire, such as is used in salmon spinning. This wire is made in various sizes and breaking strains. I experimented and found the 8 lb. breaking strain alasticum wire was best. To this I attached an eyed hook, number 8, and the best method of attaching it is as follows. (See diagram.)

This attachment ensures that the hook is not flopping

15

awkwardly on the end of the wire cast as it would if simply tied to it. The same method is, of course, employed in fly fishing when a fly is attached to a gut cast.

The smaller the float the better. You can ledger with a floatless line but such a method tries the patience of the most patient habitual carp fisher. If you have a float to gaze at, you have at least some interest; a line descending at an angle into murky waters of great depth is neither an exhilarating sight or one to foster optimism. Indeed there are great psychological deeps to be sounded in the matter of floats.

My favourite carp float is $3\frac{1}{2}$ inches long—a white quill tipped with scarlet, as every self-respecting float should be dressed and, instead of a wire or quill ring at its lower end, it is grooved and twisted so that one has only to wind the line two or three times about the 'twist' to make the float secure. The upper end is held in the usual manner by a ring to the line. The advantages of this type of float are obvious, for quick adjustment is useful in carp fishing. The float is, of course, on the line and the sinker, a single shot, is pinched on the alasticum wire at the correct depth. Plumbing your water is very necessary. The float should, of course, be at half cock, and below the shot I have at least $2\frac{1}{2}$ feet of alasticum wire attached to the hook.

When I cast out, which I do by the coiled line method, I let the bait sink and then draw the line towards me for a little way so as to allow the wire to lie along the bottom of the pool. Nothing distrubs a carp more than a perpendicular cast rising direct from the bait to the float. Your bait, needless to say, must lie on the bottom. Alasticum wire is more invisible than gut—it does not glint and is infinitely stronger.

To deal with these immensely powerful fighters, you

need strong tackle and even with the above outfit you will be lucky, in a snaggy water, if you bring your fish to bank if it is anything over 8 lbs. An 8 lb. carp is not considered any size—certainly not worthy of a glass case, if you care for mounted fish. (I would put the glass case limit at 10 lbs. at the very lowest.)

I hope, by the way, I am not boring the reader with all this dry technical detail, but it must be put down in black and white if scientific carp fishing is contemplated. As a matter of fact, interest in the species is growing. The big fellows landed in recent years seem to indicate that magnificent sport may be had if carp breeding is taken seriously. Even whilst I have been writing this chapter, there comes news of a 23 lb. carp caught at Dagenham and this Association water bids fair to rival Mapperly since several very heavy fish have been taken there in recent years. I hasten to add that the fishing is, of course, private and is in the hands of an Anglers' Association.

Carp do not often feed during the day, save on very special occasions (I am speaking still of the ledgering method). I should qualify that statement by saying they will not (as a rule) feed *on the bottom* after 9 or 10 o'clock in the morning (at midsummer) and you may not expect sport until after 7.30 p.m. B.S.T. in July. The only exception to this habit is during rough and stormy weather when you may be lucky to have bites at prolonged intervals during the day. Some hold the theory that the very big fish will not feed after sunrise, that—at the end of June—they feed almost at daybreak. I am not sure about this. One thing is certain, that they are on the move in the half light of night and may feed during the hours of darkness. But anyone expecting to hook and land a 15 lb. carp in the dark is the world's greatest optimist.

As soon as the water warms up and the sun gathers power, the carp rise to the surface and spend all the sunny hours either lazily swimming about the centre of the pool in shoals (their backs frequently out of the water) or lolling inert and tilted sideways enjoying their diurnal siestas. Basking fish, however, may be tempted to take floating crust. I have tried this method with success and it can be very killing in the right water. It all depends if the fish have been fed by having crusts thrown in to them. This brings me to a very important point. It is essential that the carp fisher, on first trying a water unfamiliar to him, ascertains if he can what the 'locals' use for bait. Carp are educated to certain baits. In some waters potato is lure—the fish will look at nothing else. In others, lobworm, and yet another carp water will have to be fished with honey paste.

I think there is a lot of rubbish written about honey paste. I do not believe that more big carp are caught on honey paste than ordinary paste in a 'paste' carp water— at least that is my experience. The size of the paste ball is important. If you are trying for the specimen fish, small balls of paste will attract small fish and other species such as roach. The size should be, generally speaking, as large as a walnut, certainly no smaller. Buckley fishes with a ball the size of a swelled pea. Perhaps that is the correct size for Mapperly. It certainly is not for my Devon locality. There the small ball of paste will bring you 1 to 3 lb. fish but the grandfathers need a larger mouthful.

In my pool in my garden I have half a dozen carp and it is interesting to see how they take the bread balls I throw to them. They are truly 'wild' fish, taken from a local lake and weigh something in the region of 2 lbs. apiece— small carp. When I throw in the bait they swim up to it very slowly—a carp is a suspicious fish—they gradually approach it and then regard it for some time before making up their minds to take it. They then gently tip up their tails, suck in the bait and instantly expel it again. They do this, on an average, two or three times. Then they swallow it. As they do so they turn with great speed and dash away for the shelter of the lilies. This is exactly what the big carp do in their true wild state. I am sure of this, and it is their cautious 'mouthing' of the bait which accounts for those gentle stirrings of the float which frequently presage a 'take'. If they feel anything *hard* or unnatural in the paste during this cautious and suspicious investigation, they will leave it and return no more.

Ground baiting is essential; a pitch should be baited up for at least a week before commencing operations and this is especially important when the pool is rarely fished. The most trying type of carp water is that which has not been fished for years, indeed such places present great difficulty. The carp have been accustomed to find their own wild, natural foods and a very long period of ground baiting is necessary. This is one of the reasons why carp are so difficult to catch; they are most fastidious fish, and staunch conservatives.

I mentioned just now the floating bread method. This can only be employed in hot weather when the carp are on the surface and it will hardly succeed unless the fish have been artificially fed by floating bread. I have tried it on carp in a pool where they had never been fed with bread and they ignored the bait though it drifted right amongst them. But basking carp can soon be schooled to take bread and if they have it thrown to them regularly, they soon learn that it is good to eat.

There is something savouring of unsportsmanlike tactics, however, in catching carp which have been fed artificially and all my best days have been in wild and secluded waters where the fish have never been cared for or treated as 'pets'.

In the floating method, no float is used and no cast. An eyed 8 hook is tied direct to a greased line and the crust or bread paste is pinched on the hook and the bait floated out among the basking fish. Flt.-Lt. Burton, who contributes his own experiences to this book will have something to say on this method of floating bread. The greatest difficulty is how to get your bait out to the fish. Should a breeze be blowing, this is not difficult; a small flat piece of wood is placed on the water with a leaf or paper sail attached to it. The bread is laid on the boat and the line coiled loosely and free of tangles (well greased so it will float for some time) and the 'boat' with its cargo despatched upon its way before the breeze. When it has reached the area where the carp are basking (this area is usually some way out on the pool) the bread is pulled off the raft and the 'boat' sails on, its mission completed. (Another method, which is adopted by the Dallington fishers, is to use a heavy pike float to carry the line out. But this makes some splash and the float is in many ways a suspicious object.) Flt.-Lt. Burton tells how, when a large carp sees the floating bread and is about to take it, he will swim round it once or twice and then go down wind of it, like an aircraft carrier about to fly off its 'sword fish'. Then there is a terrific rush and swirl and the fight is on. Floating bread method can be very exciting as may be imagined for the whole process, the sailing out of the bread and the 'take' of the fish, can all be seen—the whole of the 'action' takes place in full view.

When ledgering there are two types of bites. After the bait has been in position for some time, usually half an hour, a slight tremble of the quill may be noticed. Then there is a lengthy pause and again a trembling. Then the float moves steadily away with increasing speed, submerged like the periscope of a submarine. Very occasionally the float will rise after the first stir and lie flat on the water like a bream or tench bite. This means the fish has the bread ball in his mouth and has lifted the sinker from the bottom of the pond.

The line should always be coiled—one or two pulls off the reel laid beside the rod butt—so that, as the great fish gathers momentum, he feels no suspicious check or jerk.

The first rush of a very large carp is one of the most exciting 'takes' in the whole realm of piscatorial sport. Your rod, of course, will be on a rod rest on the bank and it often happens the fish will whip 15 yards of line off the reel before you can reach the butt. The very big fish will charge straight for the deepest part of the pool—they seem to be determined to put as much space between the angler and themselves as possible. Smaller fish of the 5 and 3 lb. category will do the most surprising things. Some will, when they feel the hook draw home, make a dash directly for the bank at one's feet. Others will rush parallel to the bank, possibly breaking you on some snag they know is there. If trees or bushes come down into the pond, the chances are they will make a dash for these and it needs the most powerful tackle to hold them off. Very few big carp can be turned in that first breath-taking rush of terror. Otters prey on carp and I think this habit of the fish to make a bolt for the bank is the natural action they invariably follow when pursued by these deadly enemies of the species.

There is one other method of carp fishing which some have tried with considerable success, when carp refuse to look at ledgered lines or floating bread.

This is to suspend the bait in mid-water, but in such a way as to have no line directly above the hook. A glance at the diagram will show how this may be done.

So much for method. A word as to landing nets. *These can never be too large*—a salmon landing net is ideal. No-

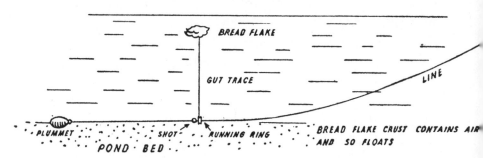

thing is more exasperating than to have a great fish help-less at your feet and only his tail within the embrace of your net. Some carp fishers gaff their fish, but somehow gaffing a carp offends the true carp fisher's feelings. Apart from that, it is not always easy to draw the gaff home in the mailed bronzed side of your victim. A mirror carp is quite a different proposition; having no such armour or few flank plates, the gaff point can find a hold but, if you intend your fish for a glass case, the less he is knocked about the better.

I forgot to mention earlier that your rod should be fitted with agate stand-off rings—at any rate the top joint ring should be of agate as smoothness and lack of 'jar' on the line (when the fish is running with the bait) are essential.

Nothing is more exasperating than to have a big fish leave you after starting his major run. This he will do if

22

he feels the slightest check—your float, racing away for the centre of the pool, will give one violent bob and you reel sadly in to find your bread paste ball or baby potato intact.

When using potato or very large balls of paste a triangle hook may be used as the bait is big enough to cover entirely the hooks and they cannot be felt when the fish take it with the mouth. Moreover, the double hold will ensure a good strike and increase your chances of landing him.

Chapter IV

HOW I BECAME A CARP ADDICT

I FIRST became interested in carp when I was about twelve years of age. I blame the writings of Mr. Shering-ham for this. In a book entitled *Coarse Fishing*, published by A. & C. Black in 1912, I read an account of how he captured his 15 lb. carp at Cheshunt. It is so vivid that I give it here.

'For practical purposes there are big carp and small carp. The latter you may sometimes hope to catch without too great a strain on your capacities. The former—well, men have been known to catch them, and there are just a few anglers who have caught a good many. I myself have caught one, and I will make bold to repeat the tale of the adventure as it was told in the *Field* of July 1, 1911. The narrative contains most of what I know concerning the capture of big carp. The most important thing in it is the value which it shows to reside in a modicum of good luck. So far as my experience goes, it is certain that good luck is the most vital part of the equipment of him who would seek to slay big carp. For some men I admit the usefulness of skill and pertinacity; for myself, I take my stand entirely on luck. To the novice I would say: "Cultivate your luck. Prop it up with omens and signs of good purport. Watch for magpies on your path. Form the habit of avoiding old women who squint. Throw salt over your left shoulder. Touch wood with the forefinger of your right hand whenever you are not doing anything else. Be on friendly terms with a black cat. Turn your money under the new moon. Walk round ladders. Don't start on a Friday. Stir the materials for Christmas pudding and wish. Perform all other such rites as you know or hear of. These things are important in carp-fishing."

'And so to my story.

' "I had intended to begin this story in a much more subtle fashion, and only by slow degrees to divulge the purport of it, delaying the finale as long as possible, until it should burst upon a bewildered world like the last crashing bars of the 1812 Overture. But I find that, like Ennius (though without his justification for a somewhat assured proceeding), *volito vivus per ora virum*. Now that a considerable section of the daily Press has taken cognisance of the event, it is no good my delaying the modest confession that I have caught a large carp. It is true. But it is a slight exaggeration to state that the said carp was decorated with a golden ring bearing the words, '*Me valde dilexit atque ornavit propter immensitatem mean Isaachius Walton, anno Domini MDCLIII.*' Nor was it the weightiest carp ever taken. Nor was it the weightiest carp of June 24. Nor did I deserve it. But enough of negation. Let me to the story, which will explain the whole of it.

' "To begin with, I very nearly did not go at all, be-

25

cause it rained furiously most of the morning. To continue, when towards noon the face of the heavens showed signs of clearness and my mind swiftly made itself up that I would go after all, I carefully disentangled the sturdy rod and the strong line, the triangle-hooks, and the other matters that had been prepared the evening before, and started armed with roach-tackle. The loss of half a day had told me that it was vain to think of big carp. You cannot, of course, fish for big carp in half a day. It takes a month. So subtle are these fishes that you have to proceed with the utmost precautions. In the first week, having made ready your tackle and plumbed the depth, you build yourself a wattled screen, behind which you may take cover. By the second week the fish should have grown accustomed to this, and you begin to throw in ground-bait composed of bread, bran, biscuits, peas, beans, strawberries, rice, pearl barley, aniseed cake, worms, gentles, banana, and potato. This ground-baiting must not be overdone. Half a pint on alternate evenings is as much as can safely be employed in this second week. With the third week less caution is necessary, because by now the carp will be less mindful of the adage concerning those who come bearing gifts. You may bear gifts daily, and the carp will, it is to be hoped, in a manner of speaking, look these gifts in the mouth—as carp should. Now, with the fourth week comes the critical time. All is very soon to be put to the touch.

' "On Monday you lean your rod (it is ready put up, you remember) on the wattled fence so that its top projects 18 inches over the water. On Tuesday you creep up and push it gently, so that the 18 inches are become 4 feet. The carp, we hope, simply think that it is a piece of the screen growing well, and take no alarm. On Wednesday,

Thursday, and Friday you employ the final and great ruse. This is to place your line (the depth has already been plumbed, of course) gently in the water, the bullet just touching the bottom so that the float cocks, and the 2 feet of gut which lie on the bottom beyond it terminating with a bait in which is no fraudful hook. This so that the carp may imagine that it is just a whim of the lavish person behind the screen (be sure they know you are there all the time) to tie food to some fibrous yet innocuous substance. And at last, on Saturday, the 31st of the month, you fall to angling, while the morning mists are still disputing with the shades of night. Now there is a hook within the honey paste, and woe betide any carp which loses its head. But no carp does lose its head until the shades of night are disputing with the mists of evening. Then, from your post of observation (50 yards behind the screen), you hear a click, click, which tells you that your reel revolves. A carp has made off with the bait, drawn out the 5 yards of line coiled carefully on the ground, and may now be struck. So you hasten up and strike. There is a monstrous pull at the rod-point, something pursues a headlong course into the unknown depths, and after a few thrilling seconds there is a jar, a slackness of line, and you wind up sorrowfully. You are broken, and so home.

' "I mention these things by way of explaining why I had never before caught a really big carp, and also why I do not deserve one now. As I have said, I took with me to Cheshunt Lower Reservoir roach-tackle, a tin of small worms, and an intention to try for perch, with just a faint hope of tench. The natural condition of the water is weed, the accumulated growth of long years. When I visited it for the first time some eight years ago I could see nothing but weed, and that was in mid-winter. Now, however, the Highbury Anglers, who have rented the reservoir, have done wonders towards making it fishable. A good part of the upper end is clear, and elsewhere there are pitches cut out which make excellent feeding-grounds for fish and angling-grounds for men. Prospecting, I soon came to the forked sticks, which have a satisfying significance to the ground-baitless angler. Someone else has been there before, and the new-comer may perchance reap the benefit of another man's sowing. So I sat me down on an empty box thoughtfully provided and began to angle. It is curious how great, in enclosed waters especially, is the affinity between small worms and small perch. For two hours I struggled to teach a shoal of small perch that hooks pull them distressfully out of the water. It was in vain. Walton must have based his 'wicked of the world' illustration on the ways of small perch. I had returned about twenty and was gloomily observing my float begin to bob again when a cheery voice, that of Mr. R. G. Woodruff, behind me observed that I ought to catch something in that swim. I had certainly fulfilled the obligation; but it dawned on me that he was not speaking of small perch, and then that my rod was resting on the forked stick and myself on the wooden box of the hon. secretary of the Anglers' Association. He almost used force to make me stay where I was, but who was I to occupy a place carefully baited for carp, and what were my insufficient rod and flimsy line that they should offer battle to 10 pounders? Besides, there was tea waiting for me, and I had had enough of small perch.

' "So I made way for the rightful owner of the pitch, but not before he had given me good store of big lob-worms, and also earnest advice at any rate to try for carp with them, roach-rod or no roach-rod. He told me of a

28

terrible battle of the evening before, when a monster took his worm in the dark and also his cast and hook. Whether it travelled north or south he could hardly tell in the gloom, but it travelled far and successfully. He hoped that after the rain there might be a chance of a fish that evening. Finally, I was so far persuaded that during tea I looked out a strong cast and a perch-hook on fairly stout gut, and soaked them in the teapot till they were stained a light brown. Then, acquiring a loaf of bread by good fortune, I set out to fish. There were plenty of other forked sticks here and there which showed where other members had been fishing, and I finally decided on a pitch at the lower end, which I remembered from the winter as having been the scene of an encounter with the biggish pike that got off after a considerable fight. There, with a background of trees and bushes, some of whose branches made handling a 14 foot rod rather difficult, it is possible to sit quiet and fairly inconspicuous. And there accordingly I sat for three hours and a quarter, watching a float which only moved two or three times when a small perch pulled the tail of the lobworm, and occupying myself otherwise by making pellets of paste and throwing them out as ground-bait.

' "Though fine, it was a decidedly cold evening, with a high wind; but this hardly affected the water, which is entirely surrounded by a high bank and a belt of trees. Nor was there much to occupy attention except when a great fish would roll over in the weeds far out, obviously one of the big carp, but 100 yards away. An occasional moorhen and a few rings made by small roach were the only other signs of life. The black tip of my float about 8 yards away, in the dearth of other interests, began to have an almost hypnotizing influence. A little after half-past eight this tip trembled and then disappeared, and so intent was I on looking at it that my first thought was a mild wonder as to why it did that. Then the coiled line began to go through the rings, and I realized that here was a bite. Rod in hand, I waited till the line drew taut, and struck gently. Then things became confused. It was as though some submarine suddenly shot out into the lake. The water was about 6 feet deep, and the fish must have been near the bottom, but he made a most impressive wave as he dashed straight into the weeds about 20 yards away, and buried himself some 10 yards deep in them. 'And so home', I murmured to myself, or words of like significance, for I saw not the faintest chance of getting a big fish out with a roach-rod and a fine line. After a little thought, I decided to try hand-lining, as one does for trout, and, getting hold of the line—with some difficulty, because the trees prevented the rod-point going far back—I proceeded to feel for the fish with my hand. At first there was no response; the anchorage seemed immovable.

' "Then I thrilled to a movement at the other end of the line, which gradually increased until the fish was on the run again, pushing the weeds aside as he went, but carrying a great streamer or two with him on the line. His run ended, as had the first, in another weed-patch, and twice after that he seemed to have found safety in the same way. Yet each time hand-lining was efficacious, and eventually I got him out into the strip of clear water, where the fight was an easier affair, though by no means won. It took, I suppose, from fifteen to twenty minutes before I saw a big bronze side turn over, and was able to get about half the fish into my absurdly small net. Luckily, by this time he had no kick left in him, and I dragged him safely up the bank and fell upon him. What he weighed I had no idea,

30

but I put him at about 12 pounds, with a humble hope that he might be more. At any rate, he had made a fight that would have been considered very fair in a 12 pound salmon, the power of his runs being certainly no less and the pace of them quite as great. On the tackle I was using, however, a salmon would have fought longer.

' "The fish knocked on the head, I was satisfied, packed up my tackle, and went off to see what the other angler had done. So far he had not had a bite, but he meant to go on as long as he could see, and hoped to meet me at the train. He did not do so, for a very good reason: he was at about that moment engaged in a grim battle in the darkness with a fish that proved ultimately to be 1 ounce heavier than mine, which, weighed on the scales at the keeper's cottage, was 16 pounds 5 ounces. As I owe him my fish, because it was by his advice I put on the strong cast, and the bait was one of his lobworms, he might fairly claim the brace. And he would deserve them, because he is a real carp-fisher, and has taken great pains to bring about his success. For myself—well, luck attends the undeserving now and then. One of them has the grace to be thankful."

'So much for what I know about catching big carp. In *fishing* for them, however, I am somewhat better instructed. I can number a good many solemn days spent in the business, and I can recall just a few bites, which invariably preceded calamity. Once, I remember, a stout new grilse-cast parted in the middle owing to the exertions of a great fish which seized a small potato. Probably there was a flaw in the gut, but I was not aware of it, and till I caught the carp of my story I assumed that breakage was the natural sequel to hooking a fish of over 10 pounds. I went in terror of these fish.

'Terror, however, adds a zest to angling, and carp fishing has always made a strong appeal to me. There is a placidity about it which you find in no other kind of angling. Having laid out your rods (you may just as well use two while you are about it, with a different bait on each), you are at liberty to smoke, meditate, read, and even, I think, to sleep, if all goes well. Nothing will happen to disturb you. You and the rods and the floats gradually grow into the landscape and become part of it. It is like life in the isle of the lotus.'

Nowadays a 15 lb. carp is not considered a really outstanding fish though few anglers can boast of having captured a fifteen pounder. But Sheringham's account fired my imagination. I immediately began to find out if there were any carp ponds in my vicinity.

I soon found one. As it was my first 'carp' water, I will describe it. I will say at once that it contained no big fish, a five pounder was, I believe, the record for that locality.

It was a small duck pond of a place, about half an acre in extent, set away behind a farmhouse in remote fields in Northamptonshire. To reach it one had to follow a rutty lane over four or five fields. The pond was in a hollow. On its south side there was an orchard with the apple trees hanging over the green shallow water. In the late summer the apples fell off the boughs and plopped into the pond, presumably to be eaten by the carp. A farm boy told me he had caught carp on small apples! On the north side was the farm and cart track and at the western end there was a brick wall which was lapped by the water. Ducks frequently disported on the pond and in hot weather pigs wallowed in it. I once saw an old sow and her farrow cross the pond from one side to the other which shows how shallow it was.

The carp in that place were to be caught on worms and a paste made of dough (flour and water kneaded into a ball). This dough was tenacious gluey stuff and it was not easy to make it stay upon the hook, but it was the best bait—bread paste was no use whatever.

The water was quite opaque, of a dark green colour, and in warm weather hideous plates of black scum rose from the bottom and drifted about in rafts on the slimy surface—a most unromantic carp water.

Yet I fished with zest and even went to the length of cycling over each evening for a week to bait a pitch on the 'orchard' side. I fished in the late evening and caught carp, small chubby fish of about four to the pound—once I caught a $\frac{3}{4}$ lb. fish—my best. I cannot explain why I preferred this miserable duck pond which contained no big fish to other deeper waters nearer home, where excellent roach, pike, and perch fishing was to be had.

One dry summer the pond practically dried up and some village boys, armed with sticks, waded across it and killed several fish of about 3 lbs. weight, which shows that they grow to a respectable size, even in such shallow water.

Below my home there were three large pools belonging to the Hall. The upper one was blind with reeds though it once held good pike. The middle pool was stocked with carp but was very overgrown and for a time we did not think it contained fish of any sort. The lower pool was full of perch, pike, and roach.

One autumn day—after heavy rains and storms—I was strolling along the bank of the middle pool when I spied an opening in the reeds. The latter had been flattened by the weather and the pool—some 10 feet across—was about 3 feet deep and quite clear.

I noticed something moving under the surface and soon I saw it was a fish, and that fish was a carp. It was a very big fish—I should say it weighed at least nine or ten pounds, and to my youthful eyes it was a giant.

The carp was moving round and round the pool as though seeking a way out. I could see the bold criss-cross pattern of its scales. How could I capture this prize? I had with me a little crazy Belgian .22 rifle and my only ammunition some sparrow shot. I am ashamed to say I resolved to shoot that carp but, knowing nothing about allowing for refraction—you must always aim below a fish when it is a few inches below the surface—I discharged the rifle several times directly at it. Beyond a boil in the water, I did not seem to disturb this patriarch. In a little while he was swimming leisurely round as before and I had to leave him. However, now I knew that there were big carp there, I set about scheming their downfall.

In the middle of the pond was an island overgrown with ground ivy and some big trees grew in the middle of it. One had a hole half way up which was a favourite kennel for a fox.

To reach this island one had to cross a quaking mass of mud and reeds and crawl along a perilous natural bridge in the shape of a fallen tree. Only the stoutest heart could accomplish this and the village boys never attempted the passage. However, I did so, encumbered with a fishing rod and a ball of paste. Blondin's crossing of Niagara on a wire was child's play compared to this balancing feat of mine.

Soon, however, my feet touched firm ground and I was on the island. On the far side to the natural bridge there was another fallen tree which lay over the water—its butt screened by holly bushes (I later found a wild duck's nest beneath it)—and I used to fish from this natural seat. The water below was five or six feet deep—very clear and the bottom black mud of prodigious depth.

But the white blob of paste, which I could see resting on the bottom, was never touched and small wonder as the carp would certainly see me perched on the fallen tree in full view. I never had a bite.

In the summer evenings, however, the carp were often in evidence, leaping up among the lilies, bronze and golden, to fall with an echoing splash which sent the ripples wheeling under my feet. How I longed to hook one of these magic fish! How unobtainable they seemed!

One hot summer (we seemed to have really hot summers in the 1920's) I went with my parents to stay with relatives in Berkshire.

I soon ferretted out a pool which contained very large carp indeed.

It was, strangely enough, a small pond of about an acre and a half, beside a country road, only separated from it by a low hedge. The banks were thick with chervil which rose up in a white forest all about it. I remember cycling over to the pond (having obtained permission through my uncle who knew the owner) and how vivid that picture remains in my mind! I even remember that I wore a white linen hat such as small boys of prep. school age used to wear in those days. It was a very hot July afternoon—the roads were thick with floury white dust and the blackthorn bushes exuded that unusual close perfume which is one of the peculiar scents of summer. I stood shoulder high among the chervil staring at an amazing sight.

The pond was very deep in the middle and as far as I

recollect there were few weeds. Round and round the pool —their broad backs occasionally breaking the surface like a school of porpoises—was a large shoal of carp. They ranged in size from half pounders to creatures like sucking pigs. I am sure those very big fish were in the 15 lb. category, but visions of our youth are sometimes false and I may be exaggerating. But there were, no doubt, some very large carp in that pond.

I fully expected to do great slaughter, though I could never have landed any big fish on my childish tackle, but as soon as I threw in my line the school departed into the amber depths and were seen no more.

Years after I went back to find that pool—I never did— I still hope I may do so. Ponds, especially deep ponds, do not often disappear completely and leave no trace.

After this, my interest in carp lapsed. Schooling and adolescence were upon me and all chances of fishing, either for coarse or game fish, did not come my way.

This lost interest returned in full force, and with an even greater resolve to outwit the carp, after a matter of fifteen years or so. The little boy in the white hat who stood among the Berkshire weeds in the full blaze of the summer sun was now grown up, had married and begotten a bouncing daughter. But the keenness of boyhood, the strange spell of the fish, was still with him, the desire to do battle with a grandfather carp no less urgent.

Chapter V

THE OBSESSION GROWS

NOT long since, I happened to call upon a watch-maker in a midland town to ask him to repair my wristwatch.

Robert Erskine is a biggish man, reminiscent of the Aga Khan, with horn-rimmed glasses and of contemplative and dignified mein. Somehow or other our conversation turned to fishing and, of course, to the subject of carp. Buckley had recently captured his stupendous fish and the angling papers were full of it. I was lamenting the fact that there were no good carp waters close at hand and the watchmaker smiled.

'You haven't fished Swancoote Pool then, Sir?'

'Swancoote Pool? Never heard of it!'

Erskine shrugged his shoulders—'There are carp in Swancoote as big as any in Mapperly—I've seen them!'

I was excited. I asked him where it was. He told me. It was set in remote country within twenty miles of my home.

He told me to whom to apply for permission; he described my route thither.

'And have you ever caught one there?' I asked.

He nodded—'Surely, I caught an eighteen pounder, which took me an hour to land. I had with me a friend who, when I had the fish beaten, went in after it and lifted it out. You see I only had a small net with me and I couldn't get a quarter of the fish into it.'

. . . . .

Since I intend to give a picture of each carp water I have fished, Swancoote Pool must now take its place in the gallery. A vastly different locality this from the miserable little green duck pond described in the former chapter.

I had some difficulty in finding it for it was hidden away in leafy country some miles from the nearest road. A gated track led me to it, one stifling afternoon, a week after my meeting with Robert Erskine. It was late July, the fields had lost their golden buttercup mantling—the white frothy weeds which bordered the little lane had gone to seed. In places I passed ancient shirt-sleeved men scything the lane margins, their sharpening stones stuck horizontally in their broad leather belts. The oaks were showing their end of summer green, the pastures had taken on that baked and veldt-like appearance associated with the end of a hot spell.

Your true carp water is—like the fish which inhabit it— secret and hidden. I was at Swancoote Pool before I realised this fact.

The lane dived down among trees and I smelt it before I saw it—a wild smell of water lilies and rotting water-weeds. There was a glimpse between willows of yellow water lilies and a flash of brightness. I heard the 'cluck' of a moorhen. Then I saw it—a large square pool of some

38

three acres, surrounded entirely on three sides by thick crowding trees—mostly oaks, elms and willows.

Only the southern end was clear; all round the top and sides were great beds of lilies with moorhens scurrying over the level pads. At the southern end there was a concrete dam and here the water was black and deep. The whole of the centre was clear water, unruffled by ripple, only broken here and there by the rings of fish.

The air was full of a fevered hum, of the countless myriads of insects in the trees, and the faint wild perfume of the water set the senses tingling.

Truly indeed a real carp water but alas! a difficult one to fish. The only possible place—without a boat—where it was feasible to cast a line, was from the dam and, by the appearance of the bank, many disciples of Isaak had been worshipping there. The earth was worn bare, scraps of luncheon paper were visible in the grass, a well worn path led through a wicket gate towards the dam.

These signs were unpromising. But all the same, a day or two previously I had had fresh tidings of Swancoote; a Mr. Frank Barker had written me a full account of how—years before—he had happened on the night of all nights, when the giants were in taking mood. Here is his account, which appeared in the *Fisherman's Bedside Book*.

'Swancoote Pool is a much lily-covered water of some few acres situated near an old Warwickshire village which, in my boyhood days had given me many hours of good fun with small roach, but that was all. Many anglers have wended their way there when better places have been inaccessible to them, and lying as it does, in the lap of lovely leafy country, who could blame them paying sixpence to old Mr. Thomas at the Farm and then watching their porcupine or quill for the whole of a summer's evening, while a pipe kept away the midges and gave consolation to the smoker?

'Bites were frequent enough but seldom were the roach more than three ounces and never half a pound, yet the water looked so clear and deep it enchanted those who besought it and almost instilled hopes of better things. Each summer, for these ever-so-many seasons, I have taken a few nice tench here, some good fish in the four-pound region, but apart from these, the small roach, and an odd eel, nothing else could be expected.

'Going back more years than I care to remember brings me to a sultry July afternoon when Arthur called and suggested we try the tench at Swancoote Pool, and to it (with desire for its peace rather than the fishing) we slowly cycled. Of the many baits with which tench can be caught we found lightly ledgering with wasp grub usually gave the best results and so in accordance with usual practice we soon got going opposite our favourite lily beds. The small roach troubled us less on wasp grub but several were taken before Arthur's rod refused to straighten and this was the first tench; two pounds or a little more.

'The sun had dipped behind the hills now but the sultry atmosphere was almost oppressive; just the night for tench. I rebaited and lightly cast again, drawing in a little to allow the grub to lie nicely, but for half an hour or so the old porcupine lay slantwise and was troubled not. Arthur was into another fish but could not get it up. For a few moments it was held, but very slowly and more surely went out for the lily roots and bang! the hook had gone. My reel was now spinning as the rod lay on the floodgate and exactly the same thing happened, out went the line without my ever retrieving an inch and I was broken too.

40

'It should be explained here that any fish had to be checked before it reached the lily roots—some twelve yards distant—or disaster was certain; we usually stopped our biggest tench in half this distance but not these fellows biting now. Arthur retackled with a stronger hook and gut but I put on another number twelve and we began again. Hardly had my wasp gone down when history repeated itself and in came another slack line.

' "Rare sport this," said my friend, as his float slid gently along the top towards the weeds. "Must be big eels." With his newly attached number eight hook he was a better match for his quarry this time, but even so he never got his float above the water again and the line shot back into the sycamore under which he was sitting. My friend changed his line for one of nine pounds breaking strain and in the meantime tench number two came to my net.

'It was not long, however, before the big goose quill on my right was sailing out again and my friend's light Spanish reed rod was a half-circle. But this time the fish was stopped; it bored deep and turned very slowly, took a yard or two and gave a yard back, now it was under the rod tip, then away again towards the lilies, but nicely checked with a few yards of the safety margin to spare. Ten minutes, twenty minutes, and then we saw the fish for the first time—a carp—which later weighed eleven and a half pounds.

'The roach were playing me up now and Arthur had settled under the sycamore again and as sure as before out went his old quill. Since that distant incident the writer has lost many a big salmon but never has he hoped to see a fish landed more than he did this old carp. Like the others it went away very slow but strong and forty-five minutes packed with thrills still found the fish as game as ever. Almost in the lily roots then away again and oh! so many times this happened.

'When at last the fish became more reasonable we saw its huge bulk lying ten feet below us nearly, a foot wide across the back and eyes larger than those of a dog. He rested and then away again towards the roots, then very slowly back bankwards. The landing net was useless, an outsize one was required, and after much fumbling, trying tail first, out he went once more, this time a little quieter. Arthur stopped him and he came to the surface where his huge dorsal moved about the top like the sail of a boy's yacht, leaving a wake like that of a duck.

'He submerged and took a yard of line, then another, a foot more then a few inches, got perilously near the lily roots then, with tip of the rod well up, Arthur held on. There was a slow creaking, a "zip" and the line flew back into the sycamore tree and the carp—the biggest I have ever seen—went back to his home in the lily roots.'

There, when I looked for it, was the identical sluice gate and from it came the whisper of water where the over-flow drained down the steep bank.

But then depression clouded my hopes. What chance had I to ever hook one of the patriarchs and, even if hooked, how could I hold them away from the sanctuary of the lily beds? No—this pool needed drastic weed cutting—it needed a boat—and only a few anglers should be allowed to fish it. Alas! it was a ticket water. For a paltry sixpence paid to the old man at the mill above, anyone could fish it and apparently many people had.

However, I baited up two rods—one with worm, the other with paste—and sitting on the sluice gate fished until dark with never a movement of my float. As evening came, gilding the tops of the oaks with golden light, an aged man came through the wicket gate, carrying a rod.

He settled himself down some yards away and began to fish and I went along to talk to him—to get, if possible, something of the history of Swancoote.

He answered my questions in a low whisper. He reminded me of Mr. Ransome's description of the habitual carp fisher. 'A man who fishes habitually for carp has a strange look in his eyes. I have known and have shaken hands respectfully with the man who caught the biggest carp ever landed in England. He looked as if he had been in heaven and in hell and had nothing to hope from life, though he survived, and after six years caught an eighteen pounder to set beside the first.'

Yes—it was true—Swancoote held immense fish, so terrifying that even the thought of hooking one was enough to make one blench. But he, personally, had never caught a big one. He told me of the miller who, a year or so before, had been walking in the field under the oaks. He beheld a mighty carp basking among the lilies and, having with him his 12 bore gun, he foully shot that monstrous object as it lolled in the summer sun.

It took all his strength to lift it in his arms and it was carried to the mill where it was hung up in a barn and the villagers flocked to gape and gasp and murmur with wonder. To me this was a sad story—that such a noble creature should have been so foully done to death. Its weight was never ascertained—the miller had no interest in his carp or in fishing, and eventually that great carp was fed to the pigs.

The chances of capturing one of the big Swancoote carp are very small indeed. In such a well-fished water they have grown excessively wary and the fact that there is

43

only one side where it is possible to fish is all in their favour. At one time there had been a boat on Swancoote but some wretched village boy, intent on voyage of discovery, set out aboard the craft, overbalanced and fell in. The story goes that the body was never recovered—perhaps the carp waxed fatter in consequence.

One thing I noticed about Swancoote—the sound of the carp sucking at the lily leaves. From all over the pool this strange faint 'suck sock' merged into one continuous sound—almost like the popping of broom pods. As the sun sank this concert ceased, the old man sorrowfully reeled in and plodded home and I was left alone with the gathering shadows and the ghost of the drowned boy.

I stayed until nearly midnight. Just before I left there came the sound, from the upper end of the pool, as of some heavy object falling into the water, a terrific plunging splash which echoed horribly in the luminous night. One of the grandfathers was jumping without a doubt.

Will another big fish ever be taken from Swancoote? It is doubtful. Since the day when Erskine and Barker caught their fish, the pool has grown up a good deal and more people fish there. The only hope is that some fortunate angler will be there one night when the giants are on the feed.

I have established without a doubt that the monsters, on very rare occasions at intervals of two or three years, really come on the feed. Such was the night when Barker fished it.

They seem to lose their natural caution and go ravening about the pond taking anything that comes their way. Such times usually coincide with thundery conditions. It is said thundery weather is bad for fishing. It is for other species of coarse fish but for carp it is good, especially after

44

a heavy warm thundery rain. Then is the best time of all.

It may be possible to catch a Swancoote giant on floating bread—given the right day, when the great fish are basking in supposed security right out in the centre. I have not yet tried floating bread at Swancoote.

As paste catches the small ones there, bread crust might do the trick. Barker hooked his on wasp grub—worms are useless. Perhaps the floating bread method may be successful. I mean to experiment more fully when we get some hot summer weather—such as we experienced in 1947.

But having hooked your fish, what then? How will you hold him off from the lilies in that first stupendous rush?

I am forced to the conclusion that the carp of Swancoote are now unassailable and will be there until the pond is drained or falls into irreparable decay. And so for many years yet the path through the wicket will be worn by weary feet—feet which tread so hopefully on arrival and so heavy with disillusionment on their departure. Many hours also will be wasted in earnest optimistic endeavour with ever negative results. The Swancoote carp have the advantage over us—undisputed kings of a beautiful kingdom.

Chapter VI

RICHARD WALKER'S LETTER

ONE day in January 1947 I received a most interesting letter from a man who lives near London, telling me of a small pool close to his house which contained very big carp. He had read in my *Fisherman's Bedside Book* (Eyre & Spottiswoode Ltd. 1945) of Mr. Albert Buckley's record twenty-six pounder and he had so enjoyed the book he felt he must write to me and tell me of his own experiences. He also sent me a photograph of a magnificent 16 lb. 5 oz. carp which he caught from this water together with the scale from a perfect monster which he found dead on the bank in 1946. This scale is here reproduced actual size.

I think that his account is so unusually interesting that I include it in this chapter.

'A carp pond where I fish is quite small, about an acre in extent, and badly weeded, especially when the water is low. It varies in depth and there is quite a lot of shallow

46

water, even when the level is normal. As well as weed there are also plenty of water-lily plants.

'My experience of big carp is practically confined to this water. I have caught them elsewhere, but usually accidentally and none over 8 lbs. I might mention in passing that I have caught *mirror* carp as small as $\frac{1}{2}$ lb., so I cannot believe that age has anything to do with their "scalelessness". I am inclined to believe that it is a simple recessive factor, which will of course breed true in a water

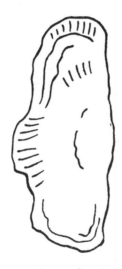

Scale of dead carp: Length $2\frac{3}{8}$ ins.; Width 1 in.

where there are no common carp, but which will gradually disappear if common carp breed with the mirror variety.

'Carp are no doubt very cunning, but they are also very greedy. Notwithstanding Mr. Buckley and other people who have caught big carp, I am convinced that anglers are mistaken in treating them as bottom-feeding fish exclusively. You are no doubt familiar with the way they

47

suck at lily leaves and surface weed—which makes a loud smacking noise. Surely this is evidence that they find a great deal of their food on the surface? All my big ones have been taken either on the surface or at the margin of the water; whenever I have ledgered on the bottom in the orthodox manner, I have caught tench, bream or rudd and only occasional carp, *never* over 4 lbs. Sometimes a bigger one is said to be hooked by a fellow-member but I set little store by these reports—people who are "smashed up" here always blame monster carp. I fancy many of these breaks are caused by carp under 6 lbs., or by big tench—I have a poor opinion of most carp fishers as anglers; they work on the principle of hold tight to rod *and* reel, pull hard and hope, and under this sort of treatment it does not take a big fish to effect a break. In fact I would say a carp of between 9 and 12 lbs. is a better fighter than the larger ones.

'We had an amusing incident last season. A new member who had come to the district from Norfolk and was therefore keen on all matters appertaining to angling, came to see me to ask how to catch a carp, and I took him down to the pond and showed him how to tackle the job, and where, on the following morning, he was to put his bait, to the *inch*. Next morning I arrived to find an unattended rod where I had indicated, *with the line round the reel-handle*. My friend was some distance away, trying to catch rudd on light tackle. So I went along to point out the danger of leaving rods with line round reel-handles, and had just finished doing so when we saw a great swirl in the water, and the unattended rod left its rest and flew through the air like a javelin—I should think it went ten yards. It dived into the water, remaining poised for a second, and then was snatched out of sight. In spite of

48

dragging operations *it was never recovered*. This is by no means the first time that rod, reel and all have been lost here, but I have never seen an outfit perform such acrobatics before.

'Sometimes these big carp jump feet out of the water, vertically upwards, and when they fall back the whole pond rocks. I have never known a hooked fish leap, however, though they will often make a great rush along the surface with their backs out of water, rising and sinking all the time like a porpoise. When hooked they go off at a tremendous pace; the reel makes a noise like a cat with its tail under someone's foot; and they go quite blindly; I have frequently known them go full-tilt into a mudbank or other obstruction and stun themselves. It is useless to attempt to stop them once they are under way, and as they usually head for weed, one must be prepared to let them have their way, but directly they enter a weed-bed, which slows them considerably, full pressure must be applied to make them fight weed and line together, which will tire them and cut up the weed-bed. Of course lily roots are a menace, and once they succeed in going round one, they are usually free fish.

'It is essential to use strong hooks, as the ordinary type soon straighten, or break, or close up. I have had an ordin-

ary crystal hook returned to me like this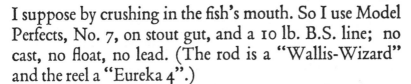

I suppose by crushing in the fish's mouth. So I use Model Perfects, No. 7, on stout gut, and a 10 lb. B.S. line; no cast, no float, no lead. (The rod is a "Wallis-Wizard" and the reel a "Eureka 4".)

'I am not fussy as regards baits; lobworms, breadcrust, paste, plum-cake, boiled potato, lily seeds (they float away when the seed-box bursts and are shaped rather like a section of an orange, with the seeds inside, but white in colour), water snail eggs (like frog-spawn but sausage-shaped and with numerous "yolks"), cockchafer grubs and wasp grub; all these have tempted ten-pounders and over. My biggest fish this year was taken on a crust, the next biggest on a bit of *plum-cake* which I took with me for my own consumption. I had another of 14 lbs. on a bit of lily-leaf with a clump of water snail eggs attached, and this same bait tempted the big one which beat me and which I guessed at over 20 lbs. I consider the size of the bait important and have no patience with people who come armed with little boiled potatoes about hazel-nut size. I use golf-ball size, and three-inch cubes of bread. A lump of paste ought to be an inch across, and worms as big as possible. A big ponderous beast of fifteen pounds is not going to bother himself to move for a pea-sized bit of dough or one miserable maggot, but he'll come right across the pond for a meal which will save the lazy brute the trouble of foraging for natural food.

'In the past I used to make a long cast with a floating bait, but now I fish a foot from the bank, either with the bait floating or on the bottom. For ground bait I mix biscuit meal or sausage rusk with diluted honey or treacle and lay a trail of it in the water as close to the bank as I can. If the weather is at all windy, this is best done where the wind is blowing against the bank—here is another matter where I am at variance with the experts, who advise fishing with the wind at one's back. This naturally makes casting easier, but why cast? I often wonder if the modern rods and reels are not making expert casters instead of expert anglers. Anyhow, the wind blows floating natural food to the bank, which I supplement with my ground bait, and the next morning I come cat-footed and drop my bait in—I find from first light until about 11 a.m. is the best time. I think evening would be as good if it didn't bring other anglers who are less circumspect, and frighten the fish out from the bank. I put my rod in a rest, of which more later, and sit on a groundsheet about twelve feet from the bank, behind a tussock or whatever other natural cover is available. Presently swirls appear near the bank—I find that the carp work along my trail of ground bait, in ones and twos, at approximately hourly intervals, always in the same direction—and as the disturbance draws nearer to my bait I always wonder whether I ought not to see my doctor and get him to check my heart over because I am convinced it shouldn't perform such antics! Eventually, if the bait is floating, a whirlpool appears round it, down which it disappears with a noise exactly like water running out of a bath. Up comes the rod, a shower of water flies in all directions, and the fun begins.

'In the case of a 16 lb. 5 oz. fish I caught, I had sallied forth on the Friday before August Bank Holiday, at 5 a.m., and on arrival at the water I found a fish moving in the weeds away from where I had baited, so I tackled up and dropped a crust among the surface weed close to the heavings, which was accepted in a minute or two, and after a bit of a tussle, during which I was shown a tail about a foot across, the fish worked into a very dense clump and sulked. Hand-lining proved ineffective, so I heaved a half brick, whereupon he surged out on the other side, the silk line parting about a foot from the hook, without any tug at the rod at all; I imagine the line was wound round the weeds a good deal; however it came back easily enough when the fish was off. All this had of course made a terrific disturbance and I wondered whether it was worth staying on, but one is always hopeful, so I went back to my baited place, where I should have gone to begin with had I been anything but a born fool, and dropped in another crust. This spot had a vertical bank with a drop of about three feet to the water, and a fringe of tall coarse grass about four feet tall which provided good concealment. Behind this I sat and hoped for two hours, during which time the pond might have been completely innocent of fish for all there was to see or hear. At about 8 a.m. another angler arrived, without seeing me behind my grass, and commenced fishing at the other end of the pond, and shortly afterwards I saw some ripples spreading out from under my bank, about ten yards along, which I thought were probably due to a rat but which I hoped might be a fish. I could not see much because of the grass, but presently the ripples came again and nearer. Then there was a big swirl and boil on the surface right under my feet, which I heard rather than saw, and the rod-tip nodded. I gave a light tap, and a great cascade of water and weed went up in the air, some in my eyes and down my neck; the reel gave a sustained high-pitched yell and things became somewhat confused; I had to get on my feet and get the water out of my eyes without letting the line go slack, but as it turned out this was not too difficult because the fish had gone about twenty yards, straight out from the bank, and buried himself in a weedy mudbank.

'Meanwhile, the other angler, hearing the splashing and seeing me rise from my grassy couch, came round at the double to see what the matter was, which was as well, because he helped me to slide down the bank in a sitting position, and passed down the net. The fish was now standing on his head, and, at intervals, lifting a quivering tail slowly into the air. Presently he began lashing it really hard, sending mud and water flying, and then came out of the mud backwards, rolled over and went straight down into the deep water, not fast but with a dull irresistible pull; he circled round on the bottom for several minutes with the line straight up and down. I put on all the pressure I could, and gradually worked him closer to the surface, eventually getting him up so that we could see him at intervals. Then he began doing vertical dives to the bottom, allowing himself to be pumped up and then rolling over and driving straight down to the bottom again; this I should think went on for nearly half an hour, without any apparent decrease in the strength of the fish, and I began to wonder whether my arm would stand much more. Each time the fish was brought to the top he would roll over before going down again so I decided to see whether he could be persuaded to dive into the net, and with this end in view, pushed it smartly out while he was rolling. He touched the rim, kicked, and then shot off towards the mudbank, but this time fate overtook him and directed his course towards an *old enamel ewer,* which stood upright, full of mud and solid as a rock, on the bottom at the edge of the bank of mud. He hit this fair and square at full speed and knocked it over, and from then on it was just a case of leading a feebly-flapping fish to the net.

'I put him in a wet sack and so home and into the bath, where he swam about until I took him out to weigh and photograph; then he was taken back and released, and swam off in a rather bewildered way. No corpse was seen in the weeks following, so I have no doubt that he recovered from his self-administered clout. It is interesting to note that the man who helped me down the bank had only caught one big one himself during the previous season, a fish of some 12 lbs. odd, yet he guessed the weight of my fish as "just under 16½ lbs." which was far more accurate than my guess, which was 14 lbs.

'The 15 lb. 12 oz. fish was caught in exactly the same way at the same spot, three days later, except that the bait was plum-cake and I had no help from the enamel jug. The tactics of the fish were the same, but this time I worked him nearer before putting out the net, and he went straight into it without touching the rim.

'The one which I like to think was over 20 lbs. behaved quite differently; he went all over the pond, not very fast but quite irresistibly and never deep until just before he broke away, or rather, shed the hook. He left channels through the weeds like those left by waterfowl and was in sight nearly all the time.

'Although the carp in this pond are undoubtedly very big, I know they are *not* very old. I have fished the water since I was four years old, and I saw the carp put in. That was about 1930, and the biggest fish put in was about 4½ lbs. Three years later I caught one of 9 lbs. on floating breadcrust. They don't seem to have bred very much, as one seldom catches a small one—only one small one, a common (not mirror) carp—was taken during 1946, as far as I know. It weighed about a pound. The tench, on the other hand, are most prolific, and small ones up to 1 lb. can be caught by the dozen. We also have bream, rudd, roach, perch, and occasional crucian carp. Before the war there were plenty of pike, but I never saw a sign of one last season. One was such a monster that I left my carp-fishing to pursue it, and eventually caught it on an 18 in. jack as livebait. It did two enormous leaps and then *literally* died. It was 38 ins. long and weighed 9 lbs., its biggest girth being round the gills.

54

'In our other water there are some fine pike and also carp, but the water is so big—about a mile in circumference, I should think—and so deep, that it is difficult to study their habits or find where they are. I caught one of 9½ lbs. there in 1937 or 1938, by accident when tench-fishing, and have seen several in hot weather, some up to 14 or 15 lbs., basking on the surface under the trees. This water contains some big perch—a club member took one of 3 lbs. 14 ozs. last summer and tells me a much bigger one followed it to the net.

'Compared with the small pond, however, it is an un-inviting water, deep, cold and clear, and it rather bewilders me, so I have never really worked hard to get a fish out of it.

'There is another pool about four miles from here, noted for its tench, which also has carp in it, one of which I saw and subsequently caught on floating crust; it weighed 8 lbs. exactly. My companion caught one of 10 lbs. next day with *five hooks to gut in his mouth*, all bright and new; I helped hold him while they were removed. This one was caught on a bunch of gentles in very shallow water.

'I am sure carp-fishers are mistaken in fishing the deep water. In your book[1] you have drawn attention to the fact that certain big carp have been caught under conditions of high wind and general rough weather. Of course. It is under these conditions, and these only, that carp in summer are found in the deep water where those anglers who caught their specimen fish were fishing. In good weather they are feeding in the weedy shallows where their natural food is in abundance, and it is there that the angler should seek them, and when he does, he will often find a muddy place where the fish are stirring up the

[1] *The Fisherman's Bedside Book*, Eyre & Spottiswoode Ltd. 1945.

bottom. Of course, if he walks round until he finds a patch of deep open water, and ledgers on its cold sterile bottom, he is unlikely to meet with much success.

'Your theory that big carp are carnivorous is most interesting. If I float a bit of bread on the surface, and small rudd come and bob it about, I stop carp-fishing and entertain myself in other angling ways, because never does a big carp feed when rudd shoals are on the move on the top. Sometimes, when the little rudd are busy with a crust, a big navy-blue form looms up and the little chaps depart in a hurry. But after a look at the bait, the carp glides quietly away and the rudd come back.

'I am enclosing a scale which I took from a carp we found very dead last summer, in June. I have no idea of its weight, as it was, as I say, *very* dead and the rats had been at it. But it was a very big one. Possibly you can deduce the age of the fish from the scale. Anyhow, it will do for you to look at after a blank day, to convince you that big carp really do exist. One begins to doubt at times!

'Before I finish I must tell you about rod-rests. I get a section of ¼ in. diameter steel rod, about two feet long, and weld some No. 8 gauge iron wire on thus:

Then bend the wire up to this shape:

so that the rod rests at the junction of the straight pieces thus:

The line is then never pinched between rod and rest, which is fatal; it runs through the rounded part quite freely, and comes clear away when the rod is lifted, without fouling. Little details are important, because two bites in a day from carp are as much as an ordinary mortal can hope for.

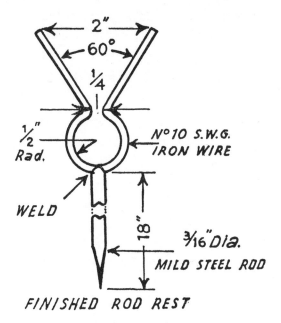

FINISHED ROD REST

'Perhaps, to conclude, I should amplify my views on baits.

'When you go trout fishing, you take great care to offer

the fish a plausible imitation of the fly on the water, or, if there are several, the variety on which the trout appear to be feeding. Failing that, there are certain flies which are killing under almost any conditions—notably Wickham and certain nondescript hackles, and these you use if the trout refuse your copy of the fly on the water, or if you are unable to offer a copy of that fly.

'I try to follow an analagous idea with carp; after rain or heavy dew, when lobworms might naturally be in the water, I use lobs. When, in August, lily leaves are adorned with water-snail eggs, I use that bait. If, due to continual heavy rain, the water has risen and covered the marginal grass, I try the cockchafer grub or the leatherjacket; and under overhanging bushes I have had fish on a fat green caterpillar. Where systematic groundbaiting has been done, paste or potato have their use. But my "Wickham" is a three-inch cube of bread, with plenty of crust, floating on the surface, and I have had more fish on this than on all the other baits put together.

'I am no believer in the theory that invisibility of tackle is important in carp-fishing; in fact, I would rather use no gut at all than gut too fine, not because of the weakness of the latter, but because the fish, not seeing fine gut, brush up against it and are thereby intimidated. 10 lb. B.S. silk line, olive green, they see clearly and fear not. The only reason I use gut is that it stands wear and tear, against weeds, bottom, and fish's mouth better than plaited silk,'

RICHARD WALKER.

Chapter VII

THE OLD COPPER MINE

WHEN I look back upon all the carp waters I have fished in my life, the old copper mine takes premier place in my affections, or rather, I should say, it exerts upon me the greatest influence, and imprints its picture most fixedly on my mind. It is a sinister place yet powerfully fascinating. You turn off the main road which hums with busy traffic, by a little thatched house as cosy as a wren's nest, its white-washed walls and latticed casements reminding one of a fairy house in a fairy wood—one almost expects a bear to be looking out of the window or a little withered witch in a steeple hat and scarlet cloak.

The winding lane (why are all the good carp waters I have known reached by little lanes?) goes up the hill, scarcely wide enough to allow the passage of a car, certainly not sufficient for two to pass each other. The strange thing is that for some years I used to visit friends of mine who lived within a few miles of Beechmere Pool (for such is its name) and I had never known of its existence!

Then that indefatigable carp fisher, Flt.-Lt. Burton,

59

wrote to me and asked whether I had ever fished Beech-mere. I looked it up on the map.

By that time my friends, a retired colonel and his family, had moved to another village in Devon, fifteen miles from Beechmere, and when I went to stay with them I naturally resolved to go to the place at the earliest opportunity and a fine business I had to find my way through the winding and tortuous little lanes with their high banks and dangerous corners. The first time I saw it, it left an indelible impression on my mind.

I followed the lane to the top where there is an old tumble-down barn and, passing through the barn yard, I still could see no sign of any pool and wondered if I had come to the wrong place. Before me the ground fell away almost sheer, clothed thickly with oaks and it was not until I descended the bank by a crooked, slippery path in the clay that I glimpsed the glimmer of the pool shining dimly through the trees at my very feet. Soon I saw its full expanse and beauty. It was a great square of dark water of about four or five acres, surrounded on all sides by high banks which were clothed on the right by oaks and on the left by magnificent beeches which came right down the steep sloping bank to the water's edge, their knotted and snaky grey roots protruding from the soil.

The August evening was overcast, not a breath of wind rustled in the trees and a deathly stillness brooded there and yet, as I listened, I realised that there was in the air a strange and fevered humming caused by the myriads of insects in the trees about. A path ran all round the pool, a slippery and dangerous path which wound its way over roots and round trees. In places it was twenty feet above the surface of the water, in others it came about level with it, evidently a fisherman's path.

60

The sloping walls of this gigantic well dived straight down into the black water—one slip upon the path in several places would have precipitated the unwary angler into unknown and terrifying depths, indeed it is said that in the middle this strange pool is two hundred feet deep.

Its history which I learned later is as follows. About a century ago it was a flourishing and busy place—a copper mine, resounding to the rumble of barrow and rattle of picks and shovels. One night the workmen went home as usual, tired no doubt with their day's work. On their return next morning an amazing transformation had taken place.

During the hours of darkness a subterranean stream had burst forth from the bowels of the mine and was rapidly flooding the whole working. Barrows and other implements were already submerged and the water won rapidly gallery by gallery until, in a very short space of time, it was full to its very brim, the stream finding an exit half way down the western side. It was beyond human ingenuity to pump the water out—indeed the whole thing had happened so swiftly and suddenly, there had been no time to combat this onrush of water and so it has remained to this day.

Some years after, a local man put in a number of carp—nobody quite knows exactly when the fish were introduced—and they have been left pretty well to their own devices. Up to a short while ago nobody fished for them save one or two locals—the postman, and an old Roman Catholic priest named Father Angelus.

Father Angelus, in shovel hat and cassock, haunted Beechmere for many years. He used to go in the very early summer mornings before other folk were astir and heaven knows what thrills he had in that shadowed place when the wood pigeon cooed among the beeches. My friend the postman, of whom more anon, frequently used to meet the priest returning from his early morning fishing, laden sometimes with a brace of carp weighing eight and ten pounds apiece. Year after year he came, so the postman said. He stayed in the neighbouring village, coming round about midsummer day and remaining until early August, going every morning to Beechmere and occasionally at night as well. I was later shown where he used to fish—right at the northern end, where the oaks overhang the black water.

And then there came a year when Father Angelus failed to put in an appearance. He has not been since. He has vanished like a migratory fish-eating bird of sombre plumage; there is no one now to wonder where he is, or how he does, or whether, like all living things, he has passed from this world. And yet—laugh if you will at my fancy—whenever I tread that winding path under the beeches at that rare hour when the world is hushed and dim, I think that any moment, at any turn of the way, I shall see him before me, tall and black in his medieval habit, burdened with basket and rod and moving with noiseless tread towards his special pitch. Though I have never met Father Angelus in the flesh, I have a clear picture of him; his presence seems to radiate a sweet kindness and simplicity, a most benevolent Spirit.

Not a fish was visible that first time I visited Beechmere; an utter stillness brooded over the place and I felt the strange and sinister atmosphere which, so the story goes, has been the cause of several suicides. I did not fish that first time—my visit was really a reconnaissance and I picked out the most likely looking spot where the water was not so deep at the southern end, and where willows crowded close round the head of the pool. Somehow too I did not feel the sinister influence there—the crowding trees did not overhang and meet above my head, cheerful moorhens flirted their white tails in the gloom of the willow thickets and passed cheerful watery remarks.

Hog weed, sturdy and strong with white umbrellas, reared in profusion from the damp grass and there was a cosy nook beside a willow bush which was firm and gravelly. In front the water deepened fairly gradually. On plumbing it I found it to be about nine feet deep twenty yards from where I decided to fish. I had taken with me ground bait in the shape of bread and worms (later I found the Beechmere carp never touched worms) and I threw this bait in, intending to come on the following morning soon after dawn.

As before mentioned, one should ground bait regularly for a week before fishing if big carp are to be persuded to take one's proffered bait, but at any rate I could make a start. In any event I only had a week in which to fish and each visit entailed a journey of thirty miles from the village where I was staying with my friends.

The next morning Beechmere seemed to have lost its sinister influence. It was a still and misty dawn, the grass wet with silvery dew, each blade wetted with pearls. Pigeons cooed among the trees and, shortly after I had set up my rod, a raven flew over 'cronk cronking'—I saw his reflection in the still mirror before me.

I approached the pitch with caution—I had put up my rod behind the massive bole of a beech—and with a good long cast I swung my ledger out a good fifteen yards beyond the willow bush. Fixing the butt in the rod rest which I had thrust into the shingle, I sat down on my seat basket, screened from the pool by a pallisade of hog weed.

I had baited with a large lump of honey paste prepared the night before. In those days I used gut casts.

Fish were on the move. Bubbles appeared from time to time, breaking all about my float, and I somehow felt the nearness of carp. For you must know that your habitual carp fisher, after many years, comes to develop an extra sense and knows when heavy fish are drawing near even though there be no bubble nor stirring of his float. He feels that gradual cautious 'drawing nearness' and almost sees the great cloudy mass, scaled like a Norman man-at-arms, materialise out of the gloom of the pond, its cunning jewelled eyes swivelling as it regards the bait with deep distrust.

But I had to wait for nearly an hour before I had a bite.

The small, white, scarlet-capped quill, which had been riding completely motionless in front of me, began to move steadily off and even as my hand gripped the cork butt of my grilse rod it was sliding out of sight and the coiled line was travelling.

This fish was a nice carp of about three pounds weight. He fought well and it took me nearly five minutes to tire him.

At that time I favoured a Hardex spinning reel with a slipping clutch but after several mishaps through the line catching on the wrong side of the guard I lost some good fish, and I later discarded it in favour of a big sea reel which held more line and was easier to manipulate.

I had several very good carp during that week—fishing morning and late evening but no really heavy fish came my way. In the week I was there—going every day—I managed to embasket about eighteen fish. These I took back to a small lake below the house where I was staying. I carried them in the seat basket, simply laying wet rushes in the bottom. The journey took me at least half an hour but when I placed the fish in the water they swam away none the worse.

The following summer, 1946, found me at Beechmere once again. The weather was not so kind—few of us will forget the wretched days, dragging on for weeks, when the rain poured ceaselessly and high winds blew. But on the whole it was a more interesting time because I connected with the monster of Beechmere.

It happened one early morning. When I reached the pool the morning was calm and still and the water, when I dipped my hand in to make some paste, was quite warm to the touch.

But after my float had been in position about an hour after sunrise, the sky grew dark and a great storm blew up. I do not think I have ever seen such rain. It drummed down in solid rods with absolute tropical fury and the wind, even in that sheltered well, lashed the surface of the pool with miniature waves. With the rain pouring off my cap and down my neck, I was reminded of one of Mr. Buckley's accounts of how he caught an 18 lb. carp on just such a wild tempestuous day and the idea came into my mind that I too might get into a big fish.

At last the fury of the storm made it impossible to remain within reach of my rod any longer so I turned to seek the shelter of a beech tree which grew on the bank close beside me.

As I did so I heard the scream of my reel. The rod was, of course, on the rod rest but so tremendous was the pull of this fish, the big reel could hardly revolve fast enough and the rod top was pulled down until it touched the water.

Two gigantic leaps brought me to the butt and, picking

65

up the rod from the rest, I tried to hold on to him. But the reel continued to scream (I had it on the check) until he had run out about eighty yards of line and was down to the backing.

I have felt the pull of a big salmon but I do not think I have ever felt such power or such an unyielding steady pull as that big fish.

He tore directly out into the very middle of the lake and then the line fell slack. I reeled in to find my cast had gone above the hook. Whether he had got me round some hidden rock deep down in the drowned galleries, I do not know, but he was gone. And then perhaps came the most impressive thing of all. By now the storm had abated somewhat and the wind had dropped a little; the surface of the pool was fairly calm.

And as I looked down the water I saw, far out in the very centre, about a hundred yards away, a slowly opening furl of ripples. It was about the size of a small table and spread and spread into one vast smooth oily patch of water which gradually died away. The great fish must have been standing almost on his head and was waving his tail in a circular motion.

I had barely reeled in my line when a voice bid me a cheery 'good morning!' and I saw, standing beside me, a postman with a bag on his back. He held in his hand a paper bag full of bread crusts which he proceeded to knead up into a massive ball of paste for ground bait.

He told me he had been baiting a pitch on the other side of the willow bush from where I was fishing and had been doing so for some weeks. He came at week-ends, fishing early, and had had some good carp in the six and seven pound category. He was able to tell me many things of the history of Beechmere—it was he who told me how the mine was first flooded and of the old priest. In July of that year (1946) we had one brief spell of hot weather and one morning he was beside the pool baiting up his pitch when he saw, basking opposite the willow bush where I was fishing, two of the largest carp he had ever seen in Beechmere and he had fished the place for close on twenty years. They lay, he saw, side by side and to get a better view he had climbed the opposite bank under the beech trees. When seen end on, he said, they were 'as wide as your seat basket, Sir' and he put their weight as well over 20 lbs. He is a good judge of the size of fish when seen in the water as he is a keen salmon fisher—indeed salmon is his real hobby and the carp take second place. Nevertheless he was a very keen carp fisher and after seeing the two leviathans he had religiously baited his pitch by the willow bush in the hope that he would connect with one of them.

I told him that I believed I had just done so and described the way the fish had taken out for the middle of the lake and how it pulled with such unbelievable power. Yes, he said, the really big fish always did that, the smaller ones usually made along the bank—undoubtedly I had got into one of the whoppers.

He looked my tackle over and voted my float too big—I should use a smaller quill and double hooks. He did not believe in letting the fish run before striking; he said the big carp in Beechmere must be struck at the first tremble of the float.

He came fishing himself next morning in his baited pitch. I had one small fish of about 3½ lbs. and after a while I heard a commotion on the other side of the willow bush and beheld him fast into a good carp. This eventually came to the net and proved to be a fish of 5 lbs. weight

—a good carp but he voted it a small one. I do not think I have ever seen such a perfect fish—broad and deep and in the most superb condition.

I noticed he baited with bread paste which was twice the size of the baits I was using—about as large as a small apple. He fished fairly close in (it was deeper water there, about eight or nine feet deep within five yards of the shore) and he used a double hook.

The following morning, fishing alone from my pitch, I was smashed by another large carp which ran at tremendous speed parallel to the bank, charging right into the partly submerged bough of an oak about thirty yards to my right. The gut cast parted as easily as did the one of the previous morning. I decided I must try some other scheme of holding these terrifying monsters. It was then my host, the colonel, suggested alasticum wire and when next I visited Beechmere I tried it out. The first result must be given in the following chapter.

Chapter VIII

EXPERIENCES WITH ALASTICUM WIRE

WHEN I reached the pool on the following morning I had great hopes of at least being able to combat the monsters. My alasticum trace had been made up the night before and an eyed 8 hook had been attached. My line—an expensive super quality black spinning line which I had used for salmon—was on the reel. I felt I had no weak link in my whole outfit. It only remained for a big fellow to give me a run. But that morning nothing conclusive was proved. I had one run from a small fish, a three pounder (it was amazing how most of the carp ran about this size) and I landed this fish in half the time it would have taken on my old gut cast method. It was useful in that it proved the fish did not see the wire—indeed, when it was lying on the dark bed of the pool, it must have been invisible.

My friend the postman came for his usual visit to ground bait his pitch—also, I suspect, to see I had not annexed it and was reaping the harvest of his labours—and during our usual morning chat he told me of an amusing adventure he had had at Beechmere many years before. Here it is.

There was a very keen carp fisher who had been baiting a pitch at the far end of the pool for some days. At that time there was a considerable area round the sides of lily beds. These have unaccountably disappeared and nobody can give the reason.

However, Jim (the postman) had some disagreement with this carp fisher (a man from 'furrin parts' and not 'a local') and though he would not tell me what the trouble was, the stranger had played him some scurvy trick and Jim meant to get his own back.

He accordingly decided to fish the stranger's baited pitch; he would get to Beechmere at daybreak and be away before his rival arrived on the scene.

This he did. It was still dark when he started out though the time was the end of June, soon after midsummer day.

I can well imagine Jim arriving at Beechmere—treading the well worn path down the bank under the great beeches where the shadows of night still lingered. It was barely light when he reached the pitch—a large pool flanked by lilies near to the place where the priest fished. The birds were just beginning to stir and the song thrushes and blackbirds to warble, as they do at that delectable time of year.

Hardly had his bait sunk when he had a run and after a stern but shortish fight, in which the carp tired to reach the sanctuary of the lilies, he brought it to bank. Luckily he had a salmon net with him and could get its bronze bulk within the folds—a magnificent carp of over 15 lbs.

Having secured his prize (and his revenge) Jim packed up and hurried away meeting his rival in the lane by the 'witch's' house. Jim told him brazenly what he had done and showed him the fish and, as Jim said, 'the language was something awful, Sir!'

The story, however, is not complete. Jim had a brother who lived up north, I think in the Leeds locality, and who was the secretary of the local fishing club.

The club wanted specimen fish to decorate its walls and had asked Jim, if ever he caught a good one, to send it along to be stuffed.

So Jim packed up his fifteen pounder and sent it off that day to Leeds. Unfortunately, his brother was away from home. His wife received the fish and, thinking it a 'new species of salmon', cut it up and divided it among her neighbours. What Jim's brother said on his return can well be imagined.

Jim was a great character and had a fund of amusing stories. His most interesting experience was when he hooked a large salmon and, after playing it for some time, it went under a sunken arch of rock and broke his line. He was at a loss what to do and, more in desperation than anything else, he cast the loose line over the floating line, which he could see trailing on the surface of the river, the salmon still being hooked. In some quite inexplicable way the loose line became entangled in the trailing line and he actually was able to land that salmon!

He found that the loose line had so twisted and tangled itself on the trailing line that it took him quite a while to undo it.

His other experience was amusing. One day a friend of his asked him if he could accompany him on one of his fishing expeditions and Jim agreed.

After a while he was into a nice fish which gave a considerable amount of trouble before it was played out. Jim then found his friend had left the gaff a long way up the river, so sent him post haste to fetch it, hanging on to the beaten fish in the meanwhile.

Time passed and still his friend did not return. Then, at last, a confused sound was heard in the distance, and he saw a whole party of people, quite fifteen or twenty, all running along the bank towards him with his friend at their head. It appeared the young fellow had been so excited at seeing a salmon hooked, he had passed on the news to a charabanc party which he happened to see by the bridge (a famous beauty spot) half a mile above and had told them to come and see the salmon caught.

The excited party then arranged themselves on a high bank above Jim where they could have a seat in the stalls as it were. One damsel sat with her legs dangling over the rock and just as Jim's friend took up the gaff there was a piercing scream from the girl who tumbled backwards among the rest of the party.

An owl, roosting below the rock, had flown out between her legs. This, however, was by no means the end of the story. Whether the girl's scream scared one of her companions I do not know but, just as Jim's friend had gaffed the salmon and was heaving it up the bank, a man fell off the rock above right on top of the salmon, knocking Jim's friend into the river. The salmon escaped back into the water and Jim's friend emerged, far down the pool, having had a good ducking.

But I fear I have strayed somewhat from the matter in hand.

The following morning I was at my pitch again, having ground baited heavily the preceding night and soon after dawn I had a run from what was apparently a very big fish. He charged up the bank towards the sunken oak

72

branch and I determined to put my alasticum wire to the test.

I held on and the line came slack and the pressure eased. Reeling in, I could not believe the wire had gone. It had not. But the *hook* had snapped just above the eye!

Unfortunately that year I did not have another chance, for the following morning, having no run at all in my favourite pitch, I moved up to the head of the pool, to the 'Priest's Hole'. After waiting an hour I had a run but the fish left the bait for some inexplicable reason. Carp will occasionally do this. It may have been it was not hungry and was playing with the bait, or his tail or some part of him had brushed against the wire trace.

So ended the season at Beechmere.

I visited this water one afternoon—not with the intention of fishing, but merely to observe the carp and I also hoped to see the two giants that Jim spoke of.

It was a warm afternoon and the fish were 'up' and basking. Standing on a little bushy knoll which overlooked the 'Priest's Hole', I could see right down into the black depths and there were about fifteen or twenty fish in view, lazing on the surface or cruising about with their backs occasionally breaking the water like a school of porpoises.

One big fish of about 10 lbs. weight was perambulating up and down a recognised beat of his. He would swim for about forty yards parallel to the bank but some forty yards out, turn about, and retrace his path, his bluish sleek back rolling into view exactly like that of a porpoise.

Others lay motionless, some end on to me. One was a very pale fish and quite distinctive from his fellows. Most were about the 3-6 lbs. mark. I did not see the giants that

73

Jim had spoken of, but they may have been at the other end of the pool.

On my last morning at Beechmere Jim brought woeful tidings. Some money-making person had bought the whole place, lake, woods and all, and was intending to turn it into a boating lido. So I doubt if I ever fish my favourite pool again.

In some ways it is (or was!) an ideal carping water, deep, shallow, very little fished, and with no weeds and few obstructions. On the opposite side to my favourite pitch however, where the beech clad banks sloped steeply into about thirty feet of water, there were several sunken trees.

I once lost a good carp there and Jim told me that it was useless to fish from that side—the very big carp always took one round one of the sunken trees and he had lost a large amount of tackle there. The 'Priest's Hole' and my pitch by the willow were, I think, the best and most likely places in the pond.

Now follows an account by Flt.-Lt. Burton, and with a graceful bow I withdraw for a space while he tells of his own experience.

Chapter IX

FLOATING BAIT METHOD

BY FLT.-LT. BURTON

THE two essential things in carp fishing are *quietness* and to keep *out of sight*. These are the only two cardinal rules that one should remember. If the fish are on the top, and they should see you, they will slowly sink out of sight, not to re-appear again for some hours, if at all. So the only way that you can hope to have any success with floating bait fishing is to be quiet, and if possible, invisible.

Spy out the water from some point of vantage until you see where the carp are lying, and then approach as carefully as you can, having put up your rod and line well away from the water. Cast out from behind a bush or from any convenient cover, if this can be done—but this is hurrying the matter too much.

Before you get to the water it would be as well to know what to take with you. Be sure at least of having a sporting chance of landing a fish, should you hook one. Personally I use a threadline outfit, with a line with a breaking strain of 4 lbs., to which I tie a hook direct on the line with a double turle knot. The hooks I use, and now treasure what few I have left, are the model Perfect Round Bend short flat shank No. 6. If the water is *free of weed,* the threadline method is deadly, inasmuch as the line, being light, helps the cast and if properly greased will float all day and is hardly noticeable on the water. If, however, and this unfortunately is more often the case than not, the water is weedy, with large beds of lilies in evidence, the best method and tackle to employ is a short ledger rod, with a good silk line of about 10 lbs. breaking strain on a *free running reel.* The hook of course would be the same as with a threadline outfit. If a silk line is used it is best to take great care with the greasing of the line, and do not use a grease which spreads a sort of 'rainbow' film on the water. Many of the proprietary brands of dressing used for line greasing at the water side have this most annoying habit. 'Cerolene,' which is a proprietary article manufacfactured by Messrs. Hardy Brothers, will float a line excellently, and has no faults. It is essential, however, to rub the line well down and almost polish it, to make sure that there are no surplus blobs of grease to detract from easy running when casting. Make sure that the reel is firmly fixed, and that the universal fittings are in no way loose. It is most annoying, and sometimes tragic, for a reel to go adrift when fighting a fish. Finally, the largest landing net that you can procure. This last item is *essential.*

We will assume that all these little points have been attended to, that we are at the waterside, that we have a fairly calm, warm day, and the fish can be seen about 15-20 ft. from the shore, basking in the sunshine—like Aldermen at a Council meeting. Carp do not shoal in the accepted sense of the word, and if there are half a dozen or more together they will be facing in all directions, and not all facing one way, as is the habit with most fish. Place on the hook a piece of crumb, from a new loaf, or as new as you can get it. A piece about as large as a big walnut. Put the hook in the bread, and pull it round until the hook is covered, and the bread is half threaded on the line, as if you were using a large worm. Just pinch the end of the bread where the line protrudes, for about half an inch, down towards the hook. Do NOT press the bread hard all over, because, remember, it has to float; *if you press it, it will sink.* Having carefully baited, dip the bread quickly in the water. This is merely to give a little extra weight. Then cast out to get the bread as near the fish as possible, but not on top of them. If you make a bad cast, and the bait arrives with a big splash, the fish will sink out of sight. In that case you just hope that they will rise again more or less in the same place; if they do not, you will have to stalk them, if they do, all well and good.

Your bait then, is out, and there is nothing you can do except wait and watch, but this waiting and watching should be done from behind a tree or any other convenient cover. If there is no cover, then lie down on the grass. Do not sit on the edge of the bank, as, if you do, you will get no fish. If the bread floats over them by a drift on the water (and even in a pond there is usually a drift of some kind), it is a moral certainty that one or other of them will take the bait. Usually what happens is that a fish will nose the bait, sink out of sight, come up on the other side, swim all round it slowly, and finally nose up to it, and take it with one huge gulp—which you can not only see, but hear. Having taken the bait, he will be off like an express train, and by virtue of the terrific rush that these fish indulge in when they 'take', it is useless to make a strike, in the accepted sense of the word. One merely picks up the rod, and when the first mad rush is over, you tighten on the line and then let it go quickly because they will be off again, and if you attempt to hold them, you will get broken every time. This is where the importance of a free running reel comes in, as with the slightest check on a 'run-away', your line is broken, however strong. I have known carp to break a line on the bite alone; they take in such a vicious way. Having hooked the fish and held him, after his first rush, the subsequent battle is governed by the condition of the water in which you are fishing. If it is impossible to turn the fish before they get in the weeds, the only thing to do is to keep a tight line and hold them. Sometimes they will come out on their own accord, but in most cases, and with carp particularly, if they get in the weeds you lose them. It is always a wonder to me how a well-hooked fish can so easily dispose of a hook when they weed you. Well, there it is then. That is the floating bait method of fishing. Obviously it is no use fishing this style if you cannot see the fish, but if you know a water well, and you are sure you can cast out a floating bait to a spot that you know *by experience* is frequented by carp, sometimes you can entice one to the surface. Sometimes a good carp water is very thick and quiet, almost stagnant in fact, and you cannot, even when the fish are on the top, see them, except for an occasional swirl. But these hints are mainly for the novice; an experienced angler can sense most of the finer points, such as have been outlined. Float fishing for carp is a very, very, very chancy business, as you may cast out in what appears to be a likely spot, and there may not be a carp within 100 yards of you, and if that proves to be the case, it is a certainty that you will not get a bite. Carp do not move around very much. How-

78

ever, if float fishing appeals, it is best not to use a float in the accepted sense of the term, so manufacture your own float from a small twig, which, when on the water, looks like a piece of driftwood. Use a strong cast, of *at least* 4x, and tie on a hook as instructed earlier. There seems to me to be no point in attaching a hook tied to a gut length to a gut cast, as this extra weakness can be avoided by tying on a hook direct to the cast. Put a very small shot, about 12 inches from the hook, and run on a small bullet on top of it, which must run freely on the line. Adjust your float for depth, so that when the bullet is on the bottom the float is lying at an angle, rather the same as in bream fishing. If the float should merely jiggle, and the odd ripple can be seen coming away from the twig, get ready to grip your rod. (I should have also said that it is advisable to pull off about 2 yards of line from the reel, and leave it lying loose on the bank.) You may get a whole series of these little taps at the float over a period of as much as half or three quarters of an hour, but finally your float will just shoot off in a flash. When this happens, your actions should be exactly as has already been outlined for floating bait fishing. In other words it is useless to strike; you merely tighten after the first rush.

Many thousands of words have been written on fancy baits for carp, and I have tried most of them at one time or another, and have gone to the waterside feeling quite happy, having procured, at some considerable trouble to myself, an exotic bait—'which they simply cannot refuse'. This is 'all my eye and Betty Martin'. New bread, fished on the top of the water, or as a ledger bait, is deadly, and the best bait that I personally know of for carp. A sweet paste made of bread and honey is also very good when ledgering, and on occasions a parboiled small new potato is excellent, but I have never got a fish with this bait. A lobworm will also, sometimes, tempt a carp to take a chance, but here again I am one of those people to whom worm fishing does not appeal, and to the best of my knowledge I have only caught one fish on a worm in my life. But I have many friends who have caught carp on the tail end of lobs.

Armed with the foregoing knowledge, therefore, which is a result of years of experience of carp fishing, any reader can go to his nearest carp pool and prove that I am wrong, on his first visit!

Carp have been caught on many peculiar baits, in fact one was reported taken last year by an angler who was spinning a minnow for trout, but I have more than a suspicion that this fish was foul hooked. They will take a fly, as often you can see them sucking them down, especially duns, and although I have tried with a fly, the flash of the cast as it drops on the water usually puts them down, so unless you wish merely to practise casting, it is not the method to use with any confidence of getting a tangible result.

Carp waters vary. You will find carp in open reservoirs, where there is no cover, no weeds, and 20, 30 or possibly 40 feet of water, which is as clear as gin. You will find carp in shallow muddy ponds where the water is foul, and where a careless step on the edge of the pond sinks you over your boot tops in stinking black mud, and where, in winter the water is frozen solid to the bottom. You will find carp in rivers. The River Parrett and Brue, in Somerset hold good heads of carp and you will find them in canals. It would appear from this, therefore, that they are not particular as to their habitat, but by experience the largest fish seem to be in a water that is deep, without being too deep, that has a good head of weed, is not subject to flooding, and has protection from real bad weather. I am firmly convinced that The Old Copper Mine, North Devon, is almost a perfect example of a typical carp water. It has that sinister air, that quiet and detached atmosphere, the deep water, the trees and the weeds, and the freedom from masses of people which carp seem to appreciate. A howling gale hardly ruffles the surface of the water, it is so well protected.

There are many, many good carp waters in England, and there are also many more abroad, especially in Austria. There is one that I know of and where I have fished, called Florida Lake, in South Africa.[1] This is a stretch of water about twice the size of Slapton, fringed in the distance with a gorgeous panorama of mountains, and is a perfect paradise scenically, and also from an angler's point of view. This water abounds with carp of enormous dimensions, and the local 'boys' spear them as and when required, which to me is a crime, but the fish are so prolific that they are classed, we must presume, as vermin. It is a beautiful spot, but very hot in summer. Whether it was the excessive heat I do not know, but when I fished there during the war (whilst convalescent near Cape Town) what fish I caught—and incidentally I never caught one under 12 lbs.—did not put up much fight, and this I attributed to the heat. I must admit that I did not feel very energetic myself, and even the excitement of catching large carp, with comparative ease, soon palled on me in a temperature which made one sweat profusely at the slightest

[1] From the Vaal River, South Africa, there are recent records of carp of 75 lbs. and 45 lbs., and a native was prosecuted for killing a carp which weighed 81 lbs. He clubbed it to death!

exertion. It was also difficult to find any shade or cover and consequently the morning and the evening were the best times to get fish.

There is another pool, Pitchford, near Shrewsbury, owned by a grand sportsman, who is a famous Severn salmon angler, that holds, so he tells me, some enormous carp. I went there on three occasions, and although conditions were ideal in every way, and I could hear the fish, I never saw one on any of my visits, but these visits of mine were not wasted, as the scenery amply repaid me for my journey to the pool, and my conversations with the generous owner, on fishing topics, made the time pass not only pleasantly, but profitably as well.

The Twickenham Piscatorial Society have (or had) a water at Bedfont, which holds some very good carp, most of which I have caught and returned, nearly all with a floating bait. There is a club at Wilmslow in Cheshire that has three small reservoirs that hold some excellent 12 lb. and 14 lb. fish, but the water is so weedy that it is difficult to land them, when hooked.

London anglers, if they care to try, have the chance of getting a big fish from the boating pond at Parliament Hill Fields, but here it is a question of fishing late at night, or very early in the morning, when there are no children, boats, dogs, etc., to keep the fish well out and on the bottom. I have a definite opinion that the fish in this pond are too well educated ever to take a bait. But big fish are there, there is no doubt of that. The Becontree Angling Society, to which I have been accorded the honour of being made an honorary Vice-President, have a water at Becontree which has yielded fish of over 20 lbs. this season, and I am assured by the Secretary that larger fish are there to be taken. I cannot give further particulars of this water, as I have so far been unable to visit it, but I shall certainly avail myself of the opportunity as soon as I can. There are carp, so I am told, in the King George Reservoir at Chingford, and they have been taken from the Thames. There is, therefore, no lack of opportunity for London anglers to try their hand at this most tantalising branch of the sport.

It may be interesting to relate a couple of personal experiences of mine, as, when one cannot fish, the best thing to do is to read, write or talk about it!

Some two or three years back, during the war, on my return from overseas, and whilst on sick leave, I went down to Sussex, and one day heard of a pond which was 'simply crawling with carp'—according to local gossip— and as these stories seemed to have the ring of truth, I thought it was worth while investigating, so I went along one day to see for myself. On arrival, I found that the 'pond' was really two ponds joined by a very narrow channel, that the water 10 feet out was only 4 or 5 inches deep, and the banks were thick black oozy mud which, when disturbed, gave off a most obnoxious smell. They were like the dew ponds one sees on Salisbury Plain, except for a fringe of reeds. In walking slowly round to see if there were any fish about, I heard some heavy splashes, and, on the far side of the pond, the water seemed to be very disturbed. I went round for a closer inspection. I found, when I got near this spot, that the water was alive with fish, and by their activities, the mud was so stirred up and mixed into the water, that it seemed to be of the consistency of thick paste, and it was impossible to see into it. On occasion, however, a broad back and fin would show itself, and I judged from these signs that the size of the fish were about 6 lbs. to 8 lbs., and there were not just one or two of them, but literally dozens. I could hardly wait to get to the farmhouse for permission to fish, which was readily granted, and the next day, which fortunately was perfect from a fishing point of view, I arrived with my usual outfit, and hoped for a good day's sport. I fished hard all day long with floating bait, on the bottom, and every other way I knew, and did not get a bite of any description, although the place was alive with carp. During the day I saw some really big fish on the move, and I could not understand why it was that I had no sport. I came to the conclusion that the water was far too thick for them to take a floating bait because when I reeled in to re-bait, the bread was quite dirty, and had turned a greyish colour, and when I fished on the bottom the bait had either been buried, or covered in half rotted leaves. The next day I decided that I would attach, about 4 inches from the hook, a small piece of cork—to keep the bait off the bottom—and this I duly did. I cast out with no shot on the line—the weight of the bread being sufficient for the cast—and before I had got my rod properly settled, I had a run. On this occasion I had not arranged my rod very well, and I did not notice that a loop of the line was round the handle of the reel, which as soon as the fish took and made his run, caught up tight on the handle, and I was broken on the bite! Undeterred, I baited again, and within ten minutes had a 6 lb. fish well hooked. I was fishing with very fine tackle and I had quite a job in manoeuvring this fish through the shallow water, near enough to net it, and nearly bogged myself in my efforts to do so, but eventually I landed it and, having weighed it, put it back. I cast out again, and within a very short time had a wonderful pull, and hooked a good fish. After playing it for some considerable time I found it was absolutely

84

impossible, and far too dangerous, to wade out for it. I was in a quandary. I did not want to lose the fish—which I knew was a good one—and it seemed to me that I could not possibly land it, the conditions being what they were. After trying various methods unsuccessfully, I made up my mind that I was going to lose this fish anyway, and it was best in the circumstances to take a chance, and try and get the fish to a spot where possibly the water was deeper near the bank. So, keeping a tight line, or as tight as I could, on the fish, I gradually eased my way round the edge of the pond until I got to a spot where the water seemed a little deeper, and again tried to coax the fish in.

I certainly got it a little nearer to the bank this time, but it was still too far out to net, and still too dangerous to wade out, so I repeated the performance, and made my way still further round the pond. By this time I was a good hundred yards from where I had hooked the fish, and still had about 35 yards of line out, but the fish was definitely weakening, and had got to the stage when, for a few minutes, he floated on his side on the surface. I could see then that he was a really good fish, and I determined I would not lose him. I again endeavoured to bring it to the bank, within netting distance, but I could not possibly find a place where this could be done. I trod down the reeds as much as I could, and stood on the resulting mat, and this gave me a little extra yardage, and got me nearer the fish, but I was still unable to reach him with the net. By this time he was nearly played out (I must have had him on over an hour), and he had very little fight left in him. I gently eased him in, floating on the surface, until at last he was within reach of my net—and then I found that he was too big to go in it! By this time I was feeling desperate, and made a last despairing effort to get him just

85

2 yards or 3 yards nearer, to enable me to lift him up under the gills. This I eventually managed to do, and I lifted him out in triumph, and turning for the bank, left one of my boots behind in the mud! I went down up to my knees in black slime, but I had the fish, which, when weighed, went over 15 lbs. Unfortunately I had killed this fish, so I could not return it, as is my invariable practice. Neither did I wish to eat it, as the smell of the mud took me a good week to get out of my system, so I gave it to a local, who was so thankful that I thought that perhaps I must have missed something good after all.

Once, whilst stationed at Taunton, I was introduced by a friend to a water which I will call The Old Copper Mine.[1] This is undoubtedly the home of record breaking fish, and many is the time that I have gone there in the hope of breaking a record, only to have my tackle broken instead.

Fishing here on one occasion, I was broken five times in the space of two hours, and, on the last occasion I was smashed, I was, in desperation, using a line of 16 lb. breaking strain, which was manufactured for pike spinning! I was amazed at the strength of these fish, and could not understand why these breakages occured, as I did everything quite ocrrectly, and took great pains not to let my excitement outweigh my carefulness, but it was no use at all. Immediately I tightened on a fish—ping! and about 30 feet of the line shot back into the trees behind me. Just imagine my feelings when I could see these enormous fish take my bait and not be able to hook and hold them. I did everything that one should do, and yet still got broken! My appetite was whetted, my blood was up. I applied for a day's leave, had it granted, and went down to try again,

[1] Beechmere.

armed with plenty of hooks and line, and two or three rods. I had planned out a method of attack, and I was certain that this time I should be successful. I was meticulously careful with everything I did, from fixing the reel to putting on the bait. I spent a pleasant day doing this, and never had a bite.

I could not visit the place again for some time, because of my duties, but at the first available opportunity, I made another visit. This time there were two local lads fishing there with pike bungs for floats, wire traces, pike hooks, and a line like a clothes line! They were letting the drift carry their bait across the pool, and they told me, in conversation, that 'they always fished this way, and it was the only way to catch fish here'. I was very sceptical of their tackle, as it was so coarse and heavy, and, I thought, if that was the only way to catch these fish, I should never get any, because I simply could not bring myself to use tackle of that kind. However, they did catch one carp of about 8 lbs. whilst I was there, so their methods did bring some measure of success. Again I had a blank day, but this did not in any way dampen my enthusiasm. To cut a long story short, each time I went to this pool I went well armed, and prepared for any eventuality; and at last, on one memorable occasion, I hooked a really good fish on a floating bait. There were no fish to be seen at all when I cast out, but I saw a few swirls on the edge of the weeds, and cast out in the hope that my bait would drift toward them. Needless to say, it did not, and floated away in the opposite direction. Being wise to the ways of carp I let it drift. It was within 2 feet of the bank, and I was sitting behind a clump of bushes smoking and watching it, when I saw an enormous fish come up and nose the bait. Knowing that within a few moments it was almost certain that he would take it, I threw away my cigarette, and got down on my knees near the rod, and awaited results. Again he came up with his tail almost touching the bait, and lay like that for at least five minutes. I was literally trembling with excitement, and eventually he slowly turned, took the bait with one huge gulp, and was off like a scalded cat. In the light of my previous experiences with these fish, I picked up my rod, and hesitated as to whether to tighten, or what to do. As I was using a threadline reel, I had the pick-up at the release position, and frankly the line whizzed off at such a speed I was too scared to push the pick-up in, in case the line went. I took the tension off the reel so that the spool ran free, and holding my breath, I pushed back the pick-up. There was a sharp jerk on the rod, and the spool whizzed round, but I felt sure that I had hooked the fish. I greatly increased the tension until the bend in the rod told me that I was almost at the limit of the breaking strain of the line, and then I started to wind. I wound, and wound, and wound, and still the fish took line. I thought that he was never going to stop. I was using a 3 lb. gut substitute line, and I had three 40 yard lengths on, behind which there was about 60 yards of old gut line.

It is amazing to me how much of this fine line one can get on a small spool. It was just as well on this occasion! To what depth he went I have no idea, but he must, without any exaggeration, have taken off at least 70 to 80 yards of my line in his first rush, before he even slackened. Then he started to bore. I hung on to that fish as though it represented all my life's savings, and gradually began to recover a little line. I started to pump him gently to get him up from the depths, and quickly recovered the line. I had had him on now for three quarters of an hour, and had not had a close sight of him since he had taken the bait, and as the water was none too clear, I had only seen his head and tail then. But I knew that he was a good fish, the best one that I had ever hooked in my life. He made various other rushes, but was obviously getting more disheartened as time went on, and the time came when he was circling sulkily within 20 feet of the bank, but still I could not see him. But at last I did manage to get his head up to the surface of the water and he lay there, 10 feet out, gently waving his tail, and looking at me with a baleful eye.

I could see then that he was a real monster, and I put his weight at quite 20 lbs., it may have been more. I eased down and got my net, flicked it open, gently slid it into the water, and held the handle with my knees while I got the fish up to a position where I thought I could lead him over it. Immediately he saw the net he was off again, and once more I lost 30 or 40 yards of line before I could stop his run. When I got him back again, he came in on his side and I knew he was nearly done. At least I thought he was. I made a further attempt to net him, but I could not get him in. He was far too big, and the leather thong across the front just sagged and he slipped out. This was the signal for him to make another despairing rush, and I really thought my line was going to part on this occasion, but it held. Again I got him back, and again he floated in on his side. He was a really lovely fish. By this time I was making bets with myself that here at last was the record breaker. And I was, in actual fact, sweating with excitement and anticipation and shaking like a leaf! Never had I seen such a carp before. His barbels were a good 2 inches long, and the mirror scales on his side looked like five shilling pieces. This I thought was the grandfather of all carp, and he was MINE! He floated in, and I tried this time to net him tail first, and do it quickly, but it was hopeless—he would not go in the net, he was far too big a fish. Two or three attempts I made, with my heart in my mouth, and each time he fell out, but there seemed no fight left in him, and he still lay where he fell each time. The water being very deep, and the banks steep and slippery, I had no idea how I could possibly land the fish, if I could not net him, other than by lifting him out under his gills. I was very tired by this time with the long battle, and the excitement, and that must be my excuse for my subsequent carelessness.

I eased him down to where the bank was less steep, and instead of going on my knees and getting my hand under his gills—as I should have done—and with one quick heave throw him up on the bank—like a fool, I tried to get him those few inches nearer by pulling on the line! I had hardly commenced to do this, before he gave just a small wriggle, and bang went the hook! And there he lay free of my line, and I looking at him with, I feel sure, tears in my eyes.

I made a despairing attempt to jam him against the side of the bank with my net, but he had just sufficient life left in him to give a couple of mighty splashes, and sink out of sight.

There is nothing further I can say about this, except that it spoiled my sleep for a month. I am certain that this fish was a record breaker, but it is no good being certain if you do not get your fish on the bank to make an uncertainty into an undeniable fact. I lost him, and that is all there is to it, but one day I hope to go back, and have another try, and if I should hook him—or one like him—I shall have a net with me big enough for any fish and myself too!

But there it is, that is one of the joys of carp fishing.

90

Chapter X

CARP GOSSIP

To grow to any size carp require deep water, but there are exceptions to the rule, as there are to every rule. Flt.-Lt. Burton has just described how he caught a 15 lb. fish out of a shallow pond, but to find a carp of this size in such a water must be of very uncommon occurrence. Sussex by the way has always been famed for its carp and in that county there are many old moats, park pools and hammer ponds where some very fine specimens are found. The species does not appear to thrive in Scotland and I have no record of any carp north of the Border. It is a fish which delights in warm weather, it also requires plenty of mud in which, during the cold spells, it semi-hibernates, though no British fish ever hibernates in the true sense, they simply become lethargic. Any rise in temperature will tempt them forth and like the tench they may some- times be caught in the depth of winter. I remember seeing a 4 lb. tench captured on Boxing Day.

Most shallow ponds, if inhabited by carp, have the

typical opaque appearance which is caused by the fish routing about in the mud. Because of this habit carp are not recommended for garden ponds, though Crucian carp do not stir up the mud so much; it is only the common and mirror carp which do so. Carp from these muddy shallow ponds are quite inedible, indeed the fish requires expert cooking to make it palatable. But from a deep clear water one can very often catch 'good eating' fish, and my friend Jim the postman has often told me he has eaten the Beechmere carp, cooking them on the bank. He wraps them in several layers of leaves and lays them in the embers. When the fish is cooked, in about ten minutes or so, he takes them out, peels off the leaves which bring the skin with them and finds the fish white, tender, and delicious.

From my knowledge of Beechmere Flt.-Lt. Burton must have found it a very difficult matter to get his floating bread out to the basking carp as the oaks overhang the water at that spot, making even ordinary casting with bait a feat of skill. On a still day there is no helping wind and even when there is a breeze the place is so sheltered hardly a ripple moves the surface. The pike float method might be successful. Some carp fishers wrap a heavy ball of ground bait around the line to make it travel out, but the ball is apt to break asunder as soon as you cast and certainly, I have found that when it hits the water, it breaks up. But if you can get it out it will also serve the double purpose of ground bait.

Personally I have never been successful with this method at Beechmere as the paste always seems to fly off the line as I throw out—there being no hook to hold it.

In any case, even with the weight of the paste, you can

never cast far enough to reach the big fish which bask in the very centre of the pool.

A clockwork toy boat has been used with excellent effect before now—the crust being laid on the deck, the toy wound up and sent on its way.

When the 'engine' runs down she will still have 'weigh' on her and will carry out your bait—if your greased line is properly coiled—and when she reaches the desired spot, the crust can be gently pulled sideways off the deck. The boat goes on (sometimes) and eventually brings up against the side of the pond. If a thread is attached, it can be pulled back. If lilies abound, you may lose your toy boat! This sounds a very childish and impracticable suggestion, but I assure the reader I have seen it done with excellent results.

I often considered using a bow and arrow but the jerk caused by the shaft leaving the bowstring will usually dislodge the crust and, unless the line is very carefully coiled, it will 'foul'. Also greased line is heavy and the boat method is far better.

Jim often fished floating bread in Beechmere and he made his boat of log with a leaf sail. Even if there is no wind a fairly heavy piece of wood—if given a good sharp push—will glide a long distance in calm water.

The slowly moving log will not disturb the carp unduly—not so much as a heavy pike float plopping among them.

It is strange that one never seems to make a great catch of carp in one day. Buckley caught four in one morning but big takes of large carp are almost unknown. In bream fishing it is possible to pull good fish from a swim one after the other, and this is also possible with tench, but not with such wise fish as carp.

I have found that, after I have landed a good one—which may have taken some ten minutes or so to bring to bank—I do not get another bite for quite an hour, usually longer. The commotion caused by the struggling fish scares all the others away. This, however, does not always apply at Mapperley, as the reader will see for himself if he reads Mr. Buckley's accounts of his experiences in that locality.

If I really set out to catch big carp I choose the following conditions.

Month—end of June or July. An early morning or late evening after a heavy warm rain (it does not matter if there is wind as long as the water is warm). Morning fishing is usually better than evening.

The best time—7 a.m. to 8 a.m. (in July) and 8 p.m. to dark. During the day you will have no sport, save a very occasional bite from a small fish. Buckley's catch of record fish in the middle of the morning was quite exceptional. He just happened to chance on a day—the 'day of days' which comes perhaps only once in a carp fisher's life—when the wiliest, heaviest fish go mad and lose their natural caution.

We do not know why fish sometimes behave in this way. Obviously it has something to do with the weather and there are probably contributory causes.

The fish have, for some reason or other, been fasting and are ravenous; it may even be sexual excitement. All fish behave in the same manner—trout, salmon, and all coarse fish. It is a matter of 'the time and place and the big fish altogether', a combination of circumstances which is in the lap of the gods.

You must remember that in carp fishing there is no constant excitement. There are long, long stretches of time

94

when your float remains immovable and without any semblance of life, but nevertheless hours which impel constant vigilance. Ransome is quite correct in stating that it is possible to 'stare a float into invisibility'. And just when patience reaches breaking point, your reel may suddenly give that urgent scream and the next few moments will be intensely exciting. No other form of fishing is like it.

The Beechmere carp—I am speaking of the big ones—differ from other fish in other waters I have angled. They do not give any warning of their approach or of their inspection of your bait. They take it on the instant, like a hungry sea trout grabs a fly, and are away in a matter of fractions of a second. Their stupendous rush is breathtaking, their power and length of run unbelievable.

I spoke just now of wind. I like a wind when carp fishing, though Jim, the postman, does not.

Any ordinary float will bob up and down in a high wind and will accordingly jerk the line and so scare any fish which are contemplating your bait—for remember that a carp will sit for some time, occasionally as long as an hour, studying your bait before making up his mind whether to reject it or no (it is usually the former decision).

Therefore, when the water is disturbed the 'Antennae' float is excellent. They ride the ripples half submerged and keep almost stationary. They are easily made. Jim recommended these floats to me and I have tried them with complete success.

Chapter XI

THE ISLAND POND

THE first time I fished the Island Pond was on 'VJ Day', 1945, an auspicious occasion.

It was evening and, as I sat on the bank upon my seat basket, screened from the pond by a wall of rushes, I heard the bells of all the little hamlets round about ringing a joyful peal. The sound of these bells coming to me beside the quiet water in that tranquil spot was very beautiful and the future seemed to hold great promise. Visions of countless other peaceful evenings beside divers carp pools seemed to stretch before me and the dark and bitter days were now surely behind.

It was very calm—very warm—an ideal evening. Swallows twittered and weaved over the willows and now and again my interest was enlivened by a great carp, rising from the pool beside the Island to fall with a hefty splash which sounded uncannily loud in the quiet.

The Island Pond merits a description and must certainly take its place in my gallery of 'carp waters'.

96

It was not large—only about one acre and a half in extent—and was virtually virgin water, that is to say, nobody ever fished it as it was on a private estate and the kind owner had given me leave to come whenever I felt like it.

In shape it was square, surrounded on all sides by willows, both silver and red barked. On the little Island in the middle grew a tall oak or two and a yew bush.

It was not a deep pond—no more than three or four feet at the deepest part—which was beyond the Island.

Incidentally, the pond was in Devon, not very far from Beechmere. Indeed, some years before it had been netted, as the owner wished to stock it with trout and he hoped to get rid of the carp—vain hope! The net broke with the weight of fish or on some hidden snag and many of the best fish escaped. A good haul was made, however, despite the accident and some very fine carp were grassed in the 10 lb. region. I believe the best was a fifteen pounder. These netted fish were taken to Beechmere, fifteen miles away.

I had tried all kinds of bait, potato (with which bait—though many carp fishers recommend it—I have never done any good whatsoever), worms, dough paste, wasp grubs and finally paste. I found that worms were the bait for the Island Pond carp. This was natural.

In an unfished water, where carp have not been educated to artificial bait, worms are your best suit, and accordingly I had laid in a supply of big lobworms. But still, that evening, I had had no bite. I had fished from late afternoon, it was now nearly 8 o'clock, and I had had no bite at all, though fish were moving all over the pond.

The Island Pool carp are the most active and exuberant of any carp I have ever seen in any water. They were, on

97

the many occasions that I visited it, always on the jump, and a fine breath-taking sight it was. My patience—like Hitler's of evil memory—was at last exhausted (this is a dreadful confession for an habitual carp fisher like myself to make) and I therefore left my rod on its rest and wandered off round the pool on a tour of inspection.

I had hardly reached the far end, and was pushing my way among the weeds, when I heard what I thought was the shrill screech of my reel. I ran round the pond and saw at once a fish was on.

The rod had been pulled into the water and the line, a rigid, straining line, stretched from the top agate under some willow bushes about twenty yards distant.

I reeled in and found my carp was still attached, very much so, as he made another dash for the willow and, despite my holding on to him, he got me tangled up among the sunken branches.

I don't know how I got him free but I did so by rough treatment and a good slanting pressure and soon I had him in the net—not a large fish—3 lbs. or so. It is surprising how even these relatively small fish can fight, even on powerful tackle and alasticum wire traces.

But the best fish were obviously by the Island; they were always in evidence there and I prevailed on the owner of the Island Pond to lend me the little green and white boat, which was moored under the willows. Early next morning I went aboard and rowed across and soon had my line out, baiting with a large lobworm. I made the best bag of fair sized carp in an hour and a half—seven fish, the largest 4 lbs., smallest 3 lbs.

These carp were longer, more 'rakish' fish than the Beechmere fish, probably due to overcrowding and lack of food. Carp of the same length in Beechmere would have weighed double. I also fished the Island Pool in the evenings but never did so well. Whether or not it really held big fish I do not know. The owner told me he had seen very large ones basking and it is quite probable that there were one or two patriarchs as the pond was very old and the carp had been there for generations.

Though the species does well in rivers, they never seem to reach the weight of pond fish. The most renowned carp river is the Brue at Bason Bridge in Somerset. I have never fished there but some very fine carp stand to its credit and of late years it has produced some fish in the 15-16 lb. category which is a good weight for a river carp.

The Weybridge Canal was once a famed locality and I believe Mr. Otto Overbeck used to fish it. One of $19\frac{1}{2}$ lbs. is recorded from this water, caught by Mr. H. Lock-smith in 1907. Canals are certainly more suitable for carp than rivers—they delight in still or slow moving water, indeed it is rather a puzzle why they do not do better and grow to greater size in canals. Perhaps they cannot tolerate the passage of barges, yet there are now many miles of derelict canals which would be eminently suitable.

I suggest to Angling Clubs that, if they have the fishing of such places, they seriously consider stocking with mirror and common carp. In a year or two they should be having good sport though they will not be able to expect any really notable fish.

Several of the Island Pool carp, when hooked, came charging into the banks of the Island at my feet, several fish getting off in this way. Jim, the postman, told me that one day, fishing at Beechmere, he hooked one of the big fellows which did this. So quickly did it come and with such power that, before he knew what had happened, his top joint, bent over by the weight of the fish rushing underneath, snapped clean off. The fish escaped which meant an evening's work for Jim splicing the break, no difficult task, for Jim makes much of his tackle and never buys a fly if he can help it—always making his own flies. Incidentally, as a young man, he told me, he sailed 'before the mast' and later spent eight years in making a model of his ship, a sailing ship, and a very beautiful model it is— no money could buy it.

Chapter XII

CONFESSIONAL CONTINUED

THE habitual carp fisher only suffers under his affliction for three months of the year. This is a mercy. At
other times he is completely sane, able to live the life of a
prosaic human being—his dreams undisturbed—his mental balance completely normal and his meals may be taken
at regular hours.

But during those three months, that is to say June, July
and August, he is concerned with only one thing—carp.

Make no mistake, his schemes, his dreams, are not concerned with *small* carp—your true carp fisher thinks only
of the monsters.

Sitting quietly on my seat basket by the twilit waters of
Beechmere, watching the hardly visible slender white tell-
tale of my quill, I think of what is going on beneath those
dark and baffling waters. I know something of the forma-
tion of that ancient copper mine—of how, from the
southern end the pool bed slopes gradually for a space, a
slope up which men and horses once toiled, which has

known the rumble of barrows and the talk of men long gone to dust. I know that there are a series of ledges, or galleries, where the miners worked, granite steps leading down into the nether pit of the working, now two hundred feet beneath the surface. The North Sea is shallower than that in many places.

And I think of the strange life of the Beechmere carp— the huge bluish shadowy shapes of the twenty pounders, gliding so effortlessly, so slowly, about those massive drowned steps.

I doubt whether the fish ever penetrate to the deepest part, even in the severest weather.

I have stood on the little bushy knoll above the 'Priest's Hole' and looked down into that black abyss and have, at times, discerned dim shapes, like grey-blue airships, gliding effortlessly about, some ten feet down. This knoll has seen grim tragedies, as might be expected. Suicides have leapt from it into that forbidding pit.

Jim told me how one night he and his boy were fishing from the opposite bank and they stayed until it was too dark to see. When they returned next morning they met police and farmers with grapples and cords, bearing the two drowned bodies of a pair of lovers who had ended their lives in one leap hand-in-hand from the wooded knoll. Nor are they the only victims the pool has claimed.

I am not a sufferer from morbid thought, I thank Heaven, but even I, standing in sunlight above the 'Priest's Hole', have felt a weird and awful fascination as I looked down into those brooding waters.

A captain of a liner once told me that frequently people have been known to leap into the boiling wake of the ship's propellers. The Japanese student frequently sacrificed himself in the volcano's mouth. So does Beechmere affect one.

Anyone accidentally falling in at the northern end would have great difficulty in getting out. The bottom slopes so steeply and is slippery clay, the rocky banks are almost perpendicular—one would be drowned like a rat in a water butt.

The southern end is, however, more kindly and one does not have any sinister feeling—moorhens cluck and flirt their tails, and green water weeds about the shallow margins give a homely touch.

One hot summer night many years ago Jim was fishing Beechmere (he frequently fished it all through the dark hours, so he told me) and, feeling unbearably hot, he took off his clothes and swam right out over the 'Priest's Hole'. It was a courageous thing to do, but Jim has no morbid fears.

The water was beautifully warm (I have often dipped my fingers in at various parts of the pond and found it quite tepid) but over the deepest part he let his legs drop down and felt a sudden awesome chill. He hastily made for the shore.

I have fished it until it was too dark to see and, sitting alone there in that gloomy place, have heard the owls calling one to another among the beechen woods and have seen them flit, moving shadows, noiseless, from one tree's rim to the other.

On windy days one hears the rush of the topmost beech leaves and, raising one's eyes, the crests of the trees seem to be tossing and rearing. But in the deep well-like hollow all is still, not a ripple moves.

I well remember one close grey morning, soon after sunrise, when I was fishing by my willow, seeing a wraith of mist rise from the water at the southern end. It assumed the form, very vaguely, of a human person, a pillar of mist some six feet in height. This ghostly apparition held a slow and stately course right down the middle of the pond until the willow bush hid it from view.

At other times, on windless mornings, soon after sunrise, a crawling film of whitish fog steals out from the margins and glides, curling and weaving, close to the oily surface of the water to disappear when it has reached the middle of the pond.

There is little bird and animal life there and no bird song save that of wood pigeons, but then I have never been there in Spring or early Summer, for I am engaged in normal occupation and pursuits.

The only two birds of note I saw were a fine buzzard which came mewing one early morning right over the oaks behind me to alight on a withered branch of a dead tree opposite to me, where he sat for some time peering at his reflection below, and the other a kingfisher which appeared from nowhere and settled on the tapering joints of my rod but, seeing me sitting among the hog weed, flew off with a shrill whistle.

To see that brilliant gem in so dark and still a place was quite amazing.

I remarked, also, a grebe, a small circular object of fluff which forced his apparently unwelcome attention on a pair of moorhens which lived under the willow. Wherever they went, he followed after, and was repeatedly chivvied away by the cock moorhen. I think he felt lonely. Once he came to visit me, bobbing up out of the pond within thirty paces of me, and regarding me with a mixture of astonishment and terror. Then he dived, but misjudging his direction, broke surface even nearer to me. His alarm

104

was highly amusing. He let out a shrill squeal of terror and dived again, this time reappearing far down the pond.

The only animal I ever saw was a red squirrel and that only once. He sat on a beech bough and scolded me, a cheerful red sprite whose presence was very welcome to a lonely, afflicted man.

I have only once seen Beechmere in bright and breezy mood and that was when a northerly wind and bright sun transformed it.

The beeches were all silvery and stirring, even to their bases, and the usually brooding water was broken by a multitude of winking ripples which flashed brilliant stars.

When I think that its peace and mystery is threatened by one who desires to make money out of it, I am angry; yet—stay a moment—are we quite sure that Beechmere will stand for such indignity?

Boats and squealing people, litter, tea kiosks, all the vulgarity and noise of the common herd—those people who remind me so of sparrows in their cheeky and noisy ways and their love of each other's company? I confess that I would be the last man to contemplate such a scheme, knowing Beechmere as I do. Already it has claimed its victims and given half a chance it will claim more; the chances will be many.

One other incident before we say goodbye to Beechmere. Two men came once, while I was fishing there. I heard them coming afar off—noisy shoutings—stumbling steps. They sat opposite to me under the beeches talking loudly and stamping about.

First one cast in a great plummet whose plunging descent awakened the echoes round the pond and set the moorhens complaining. Then, having ascertained the depth, they began to fish.

Within two hours of their coming—despite their noise and the commotion they made, they had lost all their tackle in big fish—some diving under the roots of the drowned trees—others breaking free by their headlong flight, and the inexperienced handling of the tackle which held them.

Jim—an habitual carp fisher—surprised me by talking in his naturally loud voice without any attempt at whispering. He assured me that fish do not hear, they only feel vibrations; he had proved this by shouting at them as they lay basking close at hand.

Once, he told me, when a distant quarry was blasting, the whole pond seemed to stir with leaping carp—some basking in the lily pads sprang up as if shot—wakened rudely from their noonday siesta.

It was only natural that Jim, having fished the pond for nigh on twenty years, was full of yarns concerning the place. Many I have forgotten, alas, but one I do remember. One night he was there when the giants went mad, for as I have said, big carp occasionally go 'must' like elephants.

He and his son were there. A great thunderstorm had passed and gone and after the noise and the turbulence the great pool was sleeping once again, crocodile-like, with one eye open as it were—as is ever the case.

No sooner had their baits been thrown in than off they went and nothing, Jim told me, could hold those fish, not even his son who was using a salmon rod and salmon tackle.

It was soon over, they lost all their gut bottoms and had to go home—the only time, so Jim swore, that he had ever been broken in a straight run by the Beechmere carp.

This occurred, I believe, in the same summer as Mr. Barker's experience at Swancoote—could it have been the same night? I wonder!

106

Chapter XIII

THE COURSE OF THE AFFLICTION

ANGLERS as a race (I speak of coarse fishers only) are
naturally idle men—or shall I say that they make an
art of idling? I do not say that they are not hard working,
but in their leisure moments they dislike active physical
labour. Not very many keen gardeners or farm workers are
fishermen.

Hairdressers are perhaps the most prone to a love of fishing; grooms, publicans, and retired railwaymen (signal-
men especially), are frequently born anglers, and I must
not forget butlers and footmen. The latter never have hard
physical work and also, staying in great country houses,
and visiting others, unique opportunities occur for fishing
in untouched waters.

The great homes are gone—butlers and footmen will
no doubt soon be as scarce as blacksmiths, and the fine
tranquil lakes and ponds, set among the woods and park-
lands of the big estates, become choked with weeds, un-
cared for and unloved. And more's the pity. Yet as this

world of ours grows more entangled in its wars, its discoveries, and is deafened more and more by its noise, it may be the ranks of the followers of Isaak will grow larger—there will always be those who seek for peace and the green silences.

As I have mentioned, your true habitual carp fisher is almost unique in that he pursues his craft—or suffers most acutely from his affliction, whichever way you will have it —during the heat of summer. His memories (with those of the entomologist), therefore, are mostly pleasant sunny ones; few places are more tranquil than a wood embowered pool on a summer's evening. Also he is early astir and more than any other angler senses the beauty and unimpaired freshness of the summer dawn. He has no recollection of the wintry leaden waves chasing before a keen nor'easter such as the pike fisher remembers, when it is so cold you must stamp your feet as if in a wine press and swing your arms like a demented bear. No—there is the memory of the unbelievable scents which come to the watcher in that late hour when the sun has gone, when the heated air rises up from the fields and woods, lanes and hedgerows, when the moths click among the glimmering wild rose bushes, and the little people of the night stir secretly among the reeds. To him, when he hears the heavy splash of some big questing carp, there comes a delicious shiver to visit his spine, running up and down it like the flicker of a serpent's tongue. And how many are the noises one hears beside the water at fall of night! Some can be guessed at and mental pictures formed of what manner of creatures they are—others leave one mystified. Nor is the water really still when the sun has gone. Ever and again a ripple passes through the reeds, something patters and squeaks, lily pads stir and shudder, hidden gleams come and go. It is an hour bewitched.

And then at dawn of a summer's morning the joy one feels in one's isolation! when the grass—as someone said somewhere very happily—'looks as if it had been out all night', and there is a smell in the air which is quite indescribable, so fresh and sweet is it. The smells of night are powerful and exotic, but have a sickly greenhouse flavour—the smells of the dawn make one think of youth and all the joy of the days when time seemed to be yours for ever. There is a tender greyish light on everything, the world is hushed but fully awake.

The villages, as you pass through them, seem tenantless, the inmates of the houses dead or gone—no smoke arises from the chimneys—and you surprise the cats returning after their night's hunting and loving, true wild animals that they are. The fox, too, you may catch a glimpse of, likewise going home. The martins and swallows are awake but in July few birds will greet the dawn. They sit silently upon the road, seeming to be still dazed with the fumes of sleep, and flit into the hedges with sluggish wing. Mists smoke from the hollows by the lake—a white sea of vapour through which trees and bushes rise like strange aerial monsters, tethered by invisible cables to the earth.

You thought no wild ducks visited the lake, but at that early hour you see how wrong you were in your surmise, a string of them rises quacking from the sedges.

Rabbits, too, are much in evidence, their white scuts bobbing in the thickets. Most of the cattle are still lying down—the grass is too wet with clammy dew. Cocks crow thinly and, towards the east, the sky is a mellow promise of the day to come.

So you arrive at the bankside and quietly set up your rod and tackle and soon you have cast out and have settled down to wait. But do not expect the carp to bite very early in the morning (I am thinking of July). You may not get a run until the sun is up over yonder elms and his bright rays have dispelled the last of the smoking vapours.

But the important thing is, you will be there before the carp are looking for their breakfast, they will not feel you walking along the bank.

Bubbles rise and burst upon the surface. In a shallow pond you see the mud unfurl in an opaque cloud, sometimes beautiful in its shape—like thunder clouds rolling outwards.

This means they are devouring your ground bait thrown in the night before, and any moment your quill will signal that perhaps your hour has come, that at last that glass-case fish of your dreams has made up his mind to devour your particular ball of paste among the half dozen or so which lie around it.

Do not be depressed at the thought that few men have ever caught a big carp—that on an average only one 15 lb. fish is captured in a year in the whole of Britain—that you may be one of the fortunates is not beyond the laws of averages or of chance.

Do not be depressed at the fact that since man first began to fish with a bone hook and a wriggling worm, only one man, as far as is known, has caught a 26 lb. carp in Britain. You may, the next instant, be fast into a twenty-seven pounder and you name will be shouted from the housetops and echo again and again in countless cosy bars of riverside ale houses for many years to come.

If you are fishing a water where big fish are known to

be, do not despair, I say, and when your little quill at last sinks from sight, play him as if this were that twenty-seven pounder and with as great a care.

And if you *do* get a specimen fish, does the fever leave you? Can you then sleep on, hog-like, in the summer dawning? Will the twilit pool no longer know your presence? That I cannot tell, I have yet to catch a glass-case specimen and I have been carp fishing for thirty years.

Chapter XIV

PRIVATE PONDS

WHAT pictures are conjured up by the title of this chapter! So many have I known, and fished; how numerous indeed they are! If I could be sure of living another hundred years, in full possession of health and strength, I would like to visit and to fish every private pond of any size in all the counties from mid England to the south. I would like to write a vast and heavy tome about them, to describe each one, its character and personality, for ponds are very 'personal' things—some happy and friendly, others aloof and sinister, resenting your presence, like Beechmere Pool. Each should have a chapter—each a coloured plate. Perhaps nobody would read the book, no one would be interested, but it would be a task which would give me great pleasure.

Many of these private pools were made in Georgian times—indeed the eighteenth-century squire was very fond of coarse fishing. In those days there were few distractions and sport played a very important part in the life of the country gentleman. Friends came visiting from a distance, on horseback and by coach, and stayed for weeks together. The ladies gossiped, the men shot and fished, a not unpleasant life.

Some ponds date from monastic times—some are natural ponds, very ancient, indeed they are the most historic of them all. The strange thing is that, to me, the tarns and lochs of the north of England and Scotland have not the same attraction—they seem to me to be dissociated with human affairs, so lacking in the homely cosiness which fields and woods give to a pond in the south.

One happy pool I know is within half a dozen miles of my present home. I only wish it held big carp. It holds carp but they are Crucian, and, though these fish interest me, I cannot get the same thrill in angling for them.

However, in the bright happy days of late June, I always pay it a visit to have some sport with the crucians and with the tench too—both fish are very beautiful.

The tench are like no other tench I have ever seen. They are not, I am sure, golden tench, not the true variety at any rate, which is a very beautiful fish indeed and with vivid colouring. These fish are rosy gold but on the belly only, the flanks and back are greenish bronze. They run a fair size, up to 4 lbs., and fight well and courageously.

The crucians do not run above 2 lbs. but fight, as befits any of the blood royal—in other words, the carp family— much better than the tench. I have transferred several of these Willow Pool carp to my own pond where I feed them and pet them.

Like all carp, they seldom bite but every season I secure three or more. In 1946, fishing one sunny morning (one of the few we had), I caught half a dozen one after the other, on bread paste.

The tench and carp in the Willow Pool do not seem

113

to feed early or late—10 a.m. to midday is the best time in June—and baits, worms for the tench and paste for the crucians, though the latter will sometimes take a small worm. But it is their habit of biting which is so strange.

Only on two occasions do I remember seeing any movement of the float! I have drawn up my hook in the usual way to put on a fresh bait and have been fast into a crucian —not foul hooked of course, but caught fairly in the corner of the mouth.

I give this fact to show that fish in different waters vary in their taste and habits and methods of biting.

Nearly all the fish are caught from the sluice gate. I have voyaged forth in the boat (it is a lake of two acres) but have never caught either tench or carp when fishing from it.

There are few pleasanter ways, however, of passing a hot summer day than fishing from a boat and, if the tench and crucians won't oblige, there are shoals of gudgeon and perch to help pass away an idle day. Two swans reign on the Willow Pool—each year they bring forth a lusty brood of cygnets.

When I think of this water it is always summer, with a cloudless sky and the cattle running, tails up, tortured by the gads, golden fields of buttercups, and the dreamy whisper of the sluice at the far end. If I owned the pool, I should stock it with mirror carp; it would be an ideal water, with plenty of weed, numerous deeps and good shallows for spawning and plenty of mud. Also cattle drink it one end and in nearly every good carp water you will find a cattle drink.

I spoke just now of tench. Akin in their habits to the carp, they provide on occasion splendid sport (my best is a 5 lb. fish), and are much more beautiful than the most

114

resplendent carp. Their lines are bold and noble—indeed I consider them the most attractive of all the coarse fish. The barbel has something of the shark about him, or the tope—almost a sea fish in appearance—the perch are gay but rough and coarse of scale, the roach, rudd and bream are just 'fish' to me and nothing more, though I allow that the glitter of a roach or dace is very lovely.

But in the tench the scales are excessively neat and finely wrought, and feel soft to the touch, as soft as skin. The eyes are a beautiful orange, almost ruby in some specimens, and the dorsal fin and tail finely moulded, reminding me of a Chinese bronze.

Cautious biters, they occasionally feed as well as bream (which are bold biters), and are most gallant fighters. Their spoon-like fins act as powerful screws in the water and they will test your tackle and your skill to the utmost.

Strangely enough—as is the case with barbel—very small tench are seldom caught. Perhaps they feed only on minute aquatic life and will not look at worms until they are a year or two old.

I think the oddest pond I ever fished was a little duck pond in the middle of a flat field. It was not more than 60 yards by 30 yards and was completely bushed in by willows, very shallow—not more than 6 inches or a foot at the most and the edges only an inch or so in depth.

In the centre was a dense mat of common pond weed so that there was only a strip of open water about four feet wide all round the edges.

I was told it contained carp, so naturally, as befitted a carp addict, I decided to investigate it.

Sure enough, when I stood on the bank I heard the unmistakable kissing sound of the carp sucking among the weeds and now and again a leaf would stir.

The water was very clear but I could see no fish. Nevertheless I fixed up my rod and, without a float on my line, fished with minute brandlings.

Very soon I saw a tiny object venture forth from the cover of the pond weed, followed by other little fish and soon they were stirring the mud all round my worm. At last I clearly saw one take the worm up into its mouth (I was fishing with a diminutive hook) and the next moment I had him kicking on the bank—a tiny chubby crucian. I caught fifteen in this way and they were transferred to another pond I knew of.

But though I went again on subsequent occasions, I never caught another.

The curious part is that, in dry summers, the duck pond dried up and the little fish, buried in the mud under the pond weed leaves, waited for the coming of the autumn rains.

A year or so ago the pond was 'muddied out' by the farmer and he removed thousands of these tiny crucians.

I was told he just threw all back but, when I last visited the pond, I saw no sign of life nor did I hear any 'sucking' in the weeds.

With fish fetching the price they were in that year (1945), each fish, if kept alive and placed in a tank, could have been sold for 6d. apiece. So the farmer missed a fortune.

Artificial manures, put down by farmers and land-owners on land near ponds, have been the cause of thousands of fish being poisoned. The manure drains off into the feeding springs or streams, with disastrous results to the fish population.

Speaking of tench. I live near a very big lake where some enormous tench are sometimes caught (I had one of

5 lbs. and one of $5\frac{1}{2}$ lbs. not long ago) and these two fine specimens I placed in my rockery pool. This pool is kept fresh by an electric pump[1] which keeps a constant stream flowing into it by a waterfall at one end (the same water being used over and over again).

These two lovely creatures became very tame. I fed them regularly with lobworms and paste and kept them for two years.

One hot summer I was absent and there was nobody to switch on the pump, and when I returned I found both my big tench floating lifeless on the surface, bloated and hideous.

I have since restocked the pond but have never been able to catch another large tench.

These fish are, in some ways, as curious as carp. There will be a season or two, usually running concurrently, when good fish are caught, sometimes in large quantities, and then nobody will catch a single tench for years, when they may again be caught. Nobody knows the reason for this and I cannot attempt any explanation.

.   .   .   .   .

If your lucky star happens to be in the ascendant and you do catch a record carp (or any other fish) and wish to preserve it in a glass case, I do advise going to a taxidermist of repute. I have had no experience of Coopers who seem to have made a great reputation for themselves but I lately saw a magnificent 30 lb. pike mounted by Spicers of Leamington. This was so beautifully done and the surroundings so artistic and true to life, I was most impressed by it.

Most taxidermists have no idea of mounting fish. They

[1] See *A Stream in your Garden*, Eyre & Spottiswoode, 1948.

may make a tolerable job of the fish itself, but ruin it by the surroundings. Tufts of rush are placed at regular intervals behind the fish and some atrocious background painted in—usually a picture of a pond or lake which, from the artistic point of view, would be a poor effort even by one's maiden aunt who dabbles in 'water colour painting'.

But in Spicers' specimen the water weeds were most beautifully arranged and copied true to life and there was no ill chosen and badly executed background to mar the whole effect.

A good taxidermist must have the following qualifications. He must first and foremost be skilled at his craft and must be a first rate naturalist of the highest order. He must know how a fish or bird behaves, must be familiar with its characteristics, and must be an accomplished artist too. Most stuffed fish have to be painted and, unlike a bird which loses little of its gloss and colour, the fish has to be resorted to its former beauty by cunning varnishes and skilful use of the brush and paint box. That is why one sees so few good specimens of real artistic merit. I mention this so that anyone fortunate enough to secure a specimen fish does not have it ruined by the fish stuffer. It is nonsense to say a stuffed fish is ugly—it can be *almost* as beautiful as it was in life if properly mounted with artistic background. Spicers are expensive but, if you want a thing well done, as well done as it can possibly be, they are the people to set up your fish. Rowland Ward and Coopers must be as good, but I have seen no examples of their work so cannot speak from experience.

Chapter XV

MR. BUCKLEY'S RECORD CARP

I HAVE mentioned Mapperley in earlier chapters—of how it is the premier carp water in Britain to-day and would, if it were a public water, be the mecca of all habitual carp fishers. Though you and I cannot hope to cast our lines there, however, it will not be amiss to give here Mr. Buckley's own account of his adventures, not only of catching his record fish, but of other heavy specimens secured by him, and of his methods of securing them. I am obliged to Messrs. Eyre & Spottiswoode for permission to reprint this account from my former book, *The Fisherman's Bedside Book.*

Before reading his narrative, however, I would ask the reader to remember that Buckley was not at a disadvantage which many of us have to contend with in other carp waters—that is to say, he apparently had few obstacles, bar the pen-stock in the lake, which he mentions—no lilies or fallen trees or snags in which the great fish could rush for shelter. The water is deep and clear at the spot where he landed his catches. But all the same, despite these facts, he was fishing with ordinary roach tackle, and the highest possible praise must be accorded to his skill in handling fish of such size and weight on such flimsy tackle. He must be an expert angler and fully deserves his success. He must also be an unusually lucky man to have so many heavy specimens to his credit. Whatever the water, wherever it is, the true nature of the carp does not alter. They are always excessively cunning and their habits follow a pattern. Here then is the story.

'An angler all my life and the son of an equally keen fisherman, my opportunities of indulging in my favourite sport have been restricted almost entirely to the canals and reservoirs of the border country of Notts and Derbyshire, that is, the waters within reasonable distance of my home.

'During recent years the form of angling which has proved most attractive to me has been pike fishing, and it was this branch of the sport, which, in fact, introduced me to the Mapperley carp. My father and I have fished for pike in the waters on the Shipley Estate, and from one or another we have secured some fine fish, including one specimen weighing over twenty-two pounds.

'A fortnight or so after the opening of the coarse fish season in 1930, I was trying for pike in the Mapperley Lake, in which a small group of friends and I have secured the privilege of angling, when a companion, who was fishing for roach nearby, hooked a fish of unknown species which promptly broke him and sailed away with a considerable portion of his line and tackle. He reported the happening to me who, aware of the legend of the carp which the water contained, watched carefully what happened when my friend had renewed his gear and recommenced his efforts. Sure enough, in a very few minutes, off went the float again and for over an hour a great fish was played but was ultimately lost.

'Up to that time I had never seen a carp caught, but like a wise angler I commenced my campaign against them by reading up all I could on the subject of carp fishing, and at my very first attempt, which I made a few days later, I was successful to an extent far beyond my wildest dreams, for on that occasion I secured a brace which weighed fourteen and sixteen pounds respectively. Encouraged by this success, on the morning of my great good fortune, I reached the lake, unaccompanied, just after 9 a.m. on the 24th July 1930.

'Mapperley Lake, covering an area of twenty-nine acres, is a beautiful spot just inside the borders of Derbyshire. It lies in a valley with Mapperley village on one side and the old Shipley Hall and grounds on the other. Its waters are used for the collieries nearby and there are two more reservoirs close together on the road to Heanor, a town about two miles away. On the same estate which was once owned by the late Squire Munday, of Shipley, there are rhododendron bushes which grow profusely all over the woods and grounds, making a gorgeous sight in the summer-time.

'There had been heavy rain on the previous day, and the water which normally is very clear, was slightly muddy. I fixed up a rod, a common roach rod, and fished from my favourite place, the margin of the road which passes along the crest of the embankment, at the lower end of the lake.

'My tackle was light and fine, 250 yards of No. 1 gauge line, the breaking strain of which would not be more than 3½ lbs., while the gut of the bottom tackle was 4x gauge and No. 10 hook, just ordinary roach strength, and no more. The tackle was weighted with one small shot, just sufficient to "tip" the crow-quill float to a vertical position. The bait was a small pellet of home-made paste of brown bread and honey, almost as big as a swelled pea. Owing to the gale, with the wind blowing straight towards me down the lake, I could only fish about two yards from the embankment. At the foot of the embankment the depth of the water is great, thirty feet or so, and the slope of the wall is so steep that within a few feet of the margin a fishing depth of fourteen or fifteen feet can be found. At this depth the bait rested and before it had been in position more than five minutes the first bite was registered by a trembling lift of the float and its drift in towards the foot of the wall. That fish was 15½ lbs. and it took about an hour to bring to the net. Within another five minutes or so of the new bait being cast out there followed another tussle with a smaller fish of 11½ lbs. Following this was the least of the four carp taken during this wonderful morning, a "midget" of 9½ lbs. Then came the fish of the day. Once again, almost immediately after the bait had sunk to the depths, the float indicated the interest of a fish, and on striking gently I realised that I had hooked a carp far larger than any of my captures on previous occasions.

'Being determined to secure the prize I played it with the greatest possible care, but there were many anxious moments during the following hour and a half, for it fought magnificently. There was great similarity in the fighting tactics of all the carp. As soon as they felt the prick of the hook they tore away through the water parallel with the bank at a great pace and almost immediately turned sharply up the middle of the lake, keeping well down on the bottom. The line was torn off the

122

reel at an amazing rate. The first dash took off a good hundred yards and a check affixed on the reel made a screeching noise as the fish made for the shallow waters. The giant carp gave me an anxious time and though I suppose I ought to have changed the gut and hook which had stood so much, I had not done so.

'Fortunately that stretch of the bank is clear of bushes or other obstacles, otherwise it would have been impossible to retain control of the fish. On each occasion, and particularly in the case of the twenty-six-pounder, after the first wild run alongside the wall they made mad dashes out towards the centre of the water and it was only by the exercise of the greatest skill that it was possible to turn them in their course before they reached a wooden platform from which the main pen-stock of the lake is worked, and which projects from the surface at a distance of sixty yards or more from the embankment. After just over an hour the fish showed signs of weakening. His wild rushes covered less distance, and he began to move in circles deep down for nearly half an hour. As I was using very fine tackle I dare not put much strain on to get him to the top. At last he came to the surface near the bank where he swam around for several minutes. On the wall side there were some stones which formed an inlet pool about a yard square, but not deep enough to draw the fish into. Although I used the net on the others I could not on this one owing to his size. At last he came to the bank side where he lay inert under the straining rod point, and, with hands which I confess trembled greatly, unhitched from my coat buttonhole the point of the gaff, which fortunately I had snatched up as the fish made its first wild dash, and, taking advantage of an opportunity which the fish offered as it rolled quietly just beneath the surface, I lifted the point of the sharp hook into its shoulder.

'For some curious reason the fish hardly moved even then, but to my horror, as I dropped the rod and took both hands to the gaff, the shaft broke and the fish slid back into this small inlet pool, and lay motionless! There was nothing for it but emergency measures, and regardless of all but the fear that my prize might even then ultimately jump back into the lake and escape me, I grasped the slippery bulk with both hands, and working my fingers into the gills commenced to heave it on to the bank. It was then that he struggled violently, lashing out with his great tail, drenching me from head to foot. The other fish had been securely tied up in a large bag, but without troubling about them or the risk of damage to my rod which lay where it had fallen, I ran to the keeper's cottage nearby with my dripping prize. There it was put on the scales, but as their capacity was only $25\frac{1}{2}$ lbs. the register bumped to its limit and I knew that the fish exceeded that weight.

'Greatly (and very naturally) excited over my trophy I was undecided whether to recommence fishing or not because there was in my mind the problem of getting my prize home. Fortunately at this juncture there appeared on the road an old man from the village who remarked it was the best catch of fish he'd ever seen in his life. On telling him of my difficulty in carrying the weight of fish (which was $62\frac{1}{2}$ lbs.) to Heanor, two miles away, this good Samaritan offered to go up to the village and see whether it was possible to find some means of transport.

'While waiting I packed up and went to the keeper's house from one o'clock till about four p.m. Shortly afterwards there appeared coming down the hill the desired

124

transport in the guise of a small boy pushing a little home-made two-wheeled handcart. I packed the fish into this and we commenced our two-mile tramp over the hill to the tram at Heanor. I helped the lad over the worst part of the journey by taking the hand-cart which contained two records for the British Isles (though I did not know that till later on), one for the biggest weight of carp caught in a day, and the other for the biggest fish. I gave the lad, who was about ten or eleven years of age, a shilling, and bought him some sweets, and off he went back home with his wagon, happy in himself, little knowing how much he had meant to me for the lift.

'Upon arriving home from the tram I decided to take the big carp to Nottingham, about nine miles away, where I knew a taxidermist who would set it up for me. About eight o'clock at night I arrived at his house and showed him my capture. He weighed the fish, which was caught about one o'clock, and it scaled 26 lbs. When I told him about the other carp at home he asked me what I was going to do with them. I said I didn't know, so he asked me if I would mind if I gave them him to set up for the Nottingham Natural History Museum at Wollaton Hall. I said he could have them, so he came back with me the same night for them. They are now all preserved there in their natural forms, except the large one, which is a plaster cast, the original specimen I now have at home.

'This is the story of my great red-letter day, a day well worth remembering and equally well worth recording, and one which would satisfy most of us. But not so me! I am sure Mapperley Lake contains carp of far greater size than any of my recent captures, and one day, with the best of luck, I hope to beat my own record.

'In the summer of 1932 I had the luck to hook and

125

land my next biggest carp to the record (the one of twenty-six pounds caught in 1930).

'It was a rainy season, for prior to the capture of this carp, the week before had been a series of dull, rainy days, which reduced substantially all angling opportunities, but which had, at the same time, a definitely beneficial effect in freshening up the fishing waters of the Midlands.

'One Wednesday morning towards the end of July, the day showed some signs of being favourable, with the sun rising out of a mist, so I decided to collect my fishing equipment and with sufficient food for the day packed up, I caught the tram to Heanor, where I got off and set forth on the two-mile walk on the road, by the rhododendron woodlands, climbed the road by Shipley Hall grounds, and went down the other side to the anglers' paradise in the valley, Mapperley Lake. The time would be about 8.15 a.m. when I arrived and after looking around for a short while, I made up my mind to fish on the wall side near the spot I caught the previous carp in 1930.

'I tackled up my roach rod (the same one with which I caught the other carp) and also the line and reel—about two hundred yards of No. 1 Lincoln silk line (I never fish with less on these occasions) and a fine gut bottom fitted with a No. 10 hook, together with the usual tiny crowquill which only carried one shot to cock it. The bait used was a lump of brown bread paste sweetened with honey. No ground baiting was done, only a few bits of the paste similar to that on the hook. I never believe in baiting for carp owing to the fact it attracts so many smaller fish which continually nibble the paste off the hook. The water would be about fourteen or fifteen feet deep from here and rose to two feet or more from the top of the wall. I cast out about four yards from the embank-

126

ment and let the bait lie a good foot on the bottom. I must have sat there nearly two hours. The float never stirred during that time, so I pulled the line in to look at the bait, but this was still on, so I replaced it with fresh bait about as big as a marble. I repeated this every two hours till I was on the point of packing up for the day.

'By now, the weather, which had been warm and sunshiny all day, had broken up, the sky was cloudy and the wind began to get up, blowing straight down the lake towards me. Suddenly I noticed the float stir and gradually disappear beneath the water, similar to all the other fish that took the bait in the past. I knew then it must be a carp. I tightened the line and just touched him, for I dare not strike hard on account of such fine tackle. This one seemed to give one large circle round, then off he went with a rush straight up the lake for over a hundred yards. I kept the check on the reel, which screeched out as he made his wild dash. A kind of brake is obtained by the action of the check, but at no time do I ever touch the reel with my hand while they make these rushes. By now the thunderstorm was at its height, the wind and rain beat down upon me from the open lake. The waves were lashing over the top of the wall and I simply got drenched, but I still hung on to the rod. I've never been broken yet by any of these monster carp, so I made a vow that this one I would handle to the best of my ability and skill.

'His rushes got weaker and after the space of nearly an hour I gradually got him from off the bottom. The last five minutes or so he made circular tours around near the surface where I saw him for the first time in and out of the waves. He looked almost as big as the record one when he gradually floated in. By now I was drenched and feeling tired too, but had acquired confidence in handling them and knew how much strain on the light tackle I dare put. When I could see him ready for the gaffing stage I let him have it in the shoulder which, thank God, held him, and I hoisted him up the wall side and on to the bank. There he did a bit of floundering and after dropping my rod, I soon had him in the bag.

'It was still thundering and lightning with the wind and rain still unabated too. I looked at my watch which was about 6.30 p.m. He had given me nearly an hour's sport and excitement, but I was happy in knowing I had landed him safely, although I was soaked through in the struggle. I packed up my rod and carried him across to the gamekeeper's cottage where he bumped the scales well over nineteen pounds.

'So I think I have come to the end of my story regarding the nineteen-pound carp, and by the way, as regards the history of the carp in these waters, who introduced them, and when, I am sorry I cannot give you any definite information as regards this, but I can honestly say I am the first to have caught them on rod and line.'

So ends Mr. Buckley's stirring tale, one that will put hope and determination into the breasts of every habitual carp fisher and give him food for dreams of similar success.

That there are other carp waters which hold fish as big or even bigger than the Mapperley carp is not to be doubted. But whether there are other waters so free of weeds and obstructions is another question. It is one the carp addict must answer for himself by ceaseless investigation and an urge for exploration.

Chapter XVI

THE HAPPY ANGLER

IT is an excellent thing for a man to have a hobby which takes him out-of-doors. It is better still if he has more than one hobby. I would go farther and say it is absolutely essential for a man to have a hobby, and the more passionately fond he is of that hobby, the better will he be and the longer will he live. Many find golf absorbing—a worthy game which takes one out-of-doors and provides exercise —but golf cannot be compared with shooting, fishing or hunting. Hunting needs a lifetime's apprenticeship, one can hardly take it up if one has never learned to ride. Shooting also needs a long apprenticeship unless one is naturally gifted, and so does the skilful casting of a fly. Elderly gentlemen, who are not used to getting their feet damp and cold, look askance at wading, but anyone, if they are of the right temperament, can take up carp fishing. I must admit carp fishing cannot be a wholly satisfying pastime because its period is so short, but it is certainly an excellent way of spending a summer holiday.

129

I am fortunate in having many hobbies. I am as keen on shooting as I am on fishing and every January, whatever the weather, finds me pursuing the wild duck and geese. In early summer (until the carping season) I am interested in butterflies, and birds afford me intense pleasure and material for study all the year round.

June, July and August are non-shooting months, so my carp mania fits in well. There is no month in the year which does not hold interest for me. Writing, drawing and painting are my craft and there is no more pleasant way of earning one's living, so I am a very lucky man.

All this, you will say, has little to do with the matter in hand. I mention it because I consider that many harassed business men, thinking of a hobby, would do worse than to take to carp fishing. But they would need inexhaustible patience and a contemplative turn of mind and should also be of a philosophical disposition. The very fact that the big fish offer such a challenge to one's powers of concentration and present such a difficult problem to the angler, commends carp fishing as an all-absorbing hobby, its only drawback being the short period one may indulge in it.

Yet what better time to be out-of-doors than the summer months when our fickle climate behaves itself? And what better way can you study nature, the beauty of trees and water, the play of light and shadow, and the slow changing pattern of the months?

In late June the flowers are still fresh and beautiful. It is the loveliest of all the months. The meadows are at their best then—at haytime—the trees and hedges have not lost their freshness, the days are long.

July is usually a sultry month and the herbaceous gardens are at their best. As I pass along the lane the hollyhocks—the old fashioned and double hollyhocks are coming into bloom, valerian glows upon mellow walls, white butterflies dance over the lavender hedges. Young birds are everywhere, trusting, friendly, not having yet learned their fear of man. Do not be apprehensive of early rising. You will discover a new world and wonder how you could have ever wasted so many precious hours sleeping within four walls with so much fresh loveliness outside. Jaded appetite will return, you will come in ravenous for your breakfast, you will realise that, if any daylight hours are to be spent indoors, it is the midday hours when the noise and dust and heat, the bustle of traffic, and the hurry of feet seem most insistent.

You may take your tea in peace and quietness and then, as the sky mellows over the heavy headed elms, you will journey forth to your pool once more, 'Wallis Wizard' in hand and reel on back, and discover yet another calm and lovely world waiting to be enjoyed. No small wonder the old monks were fond of fishing. No wonder Father Angelus came for so many successive seasons to the sanctuary of Beechmere!

During the winter months you may plan your carping adventures as I do—in June it shall be that pond in Berkshire—the landlady at the Three Chubs would have found favour in the eyes of Walton, and the inn is not above twenty minutes walk through pleasant meadows to the pool.

In July it shall be that Bedfordshire lake, set in that ancient park where the cattle will be grouped under the thick oaks and the great house sits in the sun dreaming of the good days past and gone when the horse was as essential to man as is the motor car to-day.

In August—what about that Shropshire pond, set

131

among the woods and tree-clad dells, hard by the half-timbered Hall where Good Queen Bess once stayed the night and praised her lodging? The keeper's wife is a first-rate cook—your bedroom clean and cosy, the windows latticed and embowered with deep red roses. Ham and eggs for breakfast when you come in, a light midday lunch—fresh lettuce perhaps and a boiled egg—and at night after your return from wooing the great carp, a supper which a king would relish (and a hunted king did relish many a meal in this county long ago). Other localities you will explore and find, comfortable quarters in farm houses (there's nothing like a good old-fashioned farm house for comfort and good food), village inns where martins twitter under the eaves and bid you be up and stirring in time to catch the carp in the old stew pond on the vicar's glebe.

There are such places, many of them, all over Southern England. Your rich sportsman may travel north in his Rolls Royce with his fine guns and dogs and servants—you will find greater peace and far more thrilling moments in your simple pleasure, talking with simple folk who are as much a part of nature as the hollyhocks which grow about the beehives in the inn garden.

Maybe your quarters will be a mill, the windows painted white, the rooms airy and clean, a spotless table-cloth and home-cured ham, fresh brown eggs, piled rashers of sizzling bacon, and the low murmur of water to lull you to sleep. All these things can your hobby bring, but you need intelligence and a certain amount of adventure in your make-up to achieve these things. There will be failures, you must expect them. I do not forget the dirty country inn somewhere in the West country, the drunken landlord, the cheap and lazy wife—townees both of them—evil people and an evil place. But after trial and error you will in time have at your disposal a list of localities, more than you require for one season's carping. And you will return to them, these happy places, gypsy like, for many years, and each visit will strengthen the tie, each will find a re-echo in the chords of memory. The simple angler with simple tastes, true follower of Walton, is a man to be envied, he is skimming the cream from life, even in the autumn of his days, and that, you must admit, is no mean achievement.

Chapter XVII

MORE METHODS

IN setting out to fish an unknown carp water it is essential to bear in mind what I said earlier on about the habits of carp. One bait which is suitable in one water will be ignored in another. The only thing one can do is to find out

(1) if the water is fished by 'locals' and, if so, what bait they use, and

(2) if it is unfished and has not been fished for years, to discover what bait they will take. In that case 'worms' is a safe card to play. Naturally worms find their way into all ponds and it will be nothing new to arouse the carps' suspicions.

In the first instance do not be despondent if the locals never seem to catch the big fellows. The average rustic is very unintelligent in fishing matters and will be found to be using the most primitive tackle—large hooks and stout gut casts which no self-respecting carp would look at.[1] Small ones may be caught but the grandfathers will ignore such insults to their intelligence. Also your average local will not fish early or late (unless he is a poacher by nature) and the midday hours, as has been shewn, will only on very exceptional occasions provide good fish. The baits which may be used in different waters are new potatoes, about the size of walnuts, boiled until moderately soft but not soft enough to break up when you push in your triangle (a small triangle holds better and you will stand a better chance of hooking your fish). Some carp fishers prefer to peel the skin off—others peel only a little skin away, yet others leave the skin entire. Bread paste should be well kneaded but not *too tough*, not so tough as to interfere with the draw of the hook through the bait when you strike. Many carp are lost in this way. They take up the ball into their mouths and rush off with it. They feel the jerk of the strike but the hook does not pull home and they spit it out as they flee. You will never hook that particular fish again for many days.

Again, the paste must not be too soft or it will dissolve away. The greatest mistake many anglers make in fishing for carp is absurdly obvious. They pull in their bait after it has been in position for twenty minutes or so thinking the paste has either been sucked off by the carp or dissolved away. If the bait is of the right consistency, it will stay on the hook for two hours at a stretch. I usually leave my bait (on the ledger) undisturbed for at least an hour—usually an hour and a half—and when I do draw it in for renewal or inspection, I do so very slowly so as not to disturb an interested fish. How many record carp have

[1] I once caught a 10 lb. fish from Hertfordshire on stout tackle but in that case line and cast *lay* on the weeds or was suspended *above* the water

been lost by this habit of the angler's of 'fussing' with his tackle. The great fish may have been watching the bait for half an hour or more and is just about to make a 'round mouth' at your paste, when it is mysteriously drawn away and that carp has learned a lesson, and his sagacity is increased.

Jim, however, told me that, on occasion, when carp are playing with the bait (this may be seen by stealthy stirrings of the float) he has sometimes induced them to make up their mind by slowly drawing the bait towards the bank, only a few inches, and then the carp seize it. This method works sometimes in Beechmere but, as has already been intimated, what is true of one water will be useless in another.

Green peas, beans, and wasp grubs are sometimes very killing, the latter bait especially. French carp fishers use beans, lightly boiled, and in some pools this bait is excellent. A few anglers—Mr. Phillips for instance—thinks that worms are the best bait, but from long experience I cannot agree with him. I should put bread paste, sweetened or unsweetened, as the most general carp bait, but the size of the ball must be no smaller than a walnut if you wish to connect with worth while carp.

I have never done any good whatsoever fishing *off* the bottom, but that this method is successful under certain conditions such as cloudy water is proved by Burton's account.

A short time ago that excellent little *Anglers' News* published an account by a man who could do no good with carp in a pool whatever bait he tried. He was fishing on the bottom. At last he invented a method which was half-ledger, half-suspended bait, allowing the paste to float in midwater but with no line above the paste. (A somewhat similar arrangement is given in Ch. III.)

136

Burton bears this out in his experiences—he thinks (and rightly too) that the big carp will swim above the bait several times and if he feels the line, or sees it, he will go away. I am sure this is why ledgering is usually the best method. The cast (alasticum or gut) lies along the bed of the pool and there is almost invisible.

You should ground bait the night before with the bait you intend to use, if possible for some days, and when you begin to fish cast in half a dozen or so similar sized balls of paste to the one on your hook. It will take a very clever fish to 'spot the lady', i.e. the ball of paste which is armed and ready. A wasp grub, fat and living, is perhaps the most deadly of all carp baits, even in a water which has been unfished and the carp are uneducated. But the great drawback to wasp grub is the fact you must fish very fine with small hooks and light casts and, though you will have the thrill of hooking a big carp, you will never land him unless the water is clear of snags and even then your angling skill will be tried to the utmost and you must expect a long battle.

In actual fact I would be so bold as to say that more really big carp have been *hooked* on wasp grub than on any other bait. Maggot falls into this category also; I class them together. A 23 lb. carp landed at Becontree in 1946 was caught on maggot.

Another rather obvious point to remember is that the rod must never be held, it must always be on a rest. It does not matter very much if it overhangs the water when there are bushes near, but in an open bank and with 'clearish' water I would advocate keeping the butt well back on the bank.

You must always be close to the rod but never stand up; hide yourself behind reeds or bushes if you can.

137

I have frequently hooked carp when I have been absent from the rod. I have never had a bite while I have been in view, but as soon as I have gone away and left my tackle I have had a run.

Curiously enough, some time ago there was an article on carp fishing in the *Fishing Gazette*. The writer described the tremendous lengths he resorted to to deceive the fish. There was an iron gate which gave access to the particular pond and he would make a show of going down the path and banging the gate behind him as though he were homeward bound. As soon as the fish felt the jar of the gate banging to, a sound no doubt they associated with departing anglers and plentiful ground bait waiting to be devoured, they would begin to bite. Whether this story was true I do no know. For my part I never would advise advertising one's presence at all, the carp are amazingly sensitive to human presence. In Beechmere I have frequently, when descending the path to my pitch by the willow, seen the whole corner bubbling with carp which were devouring my ground bait. But as soon as I arrived on the bank side, even though I came stealthily, the bubbles died away and not a movement of the fish was seen. They had all been aware of my arrival and had departed.

Once you can get carp to eat your ground bait you are of course half way to success, but all the same, as already stated, I do not believe the huge carp feed frequently, they are like big pike in this respect. You will no doubt have sport with 3 lb.-6 lb. fish (and very high class fun it is), but the patriarchs of the tribe do not mingle with the common herd but keep apart. They feed apart and bask apart, usually singly or in pairs.

The biggest fish I watched at Beechmere were never

with the main shoals, they seemed to possess a lonely dig-
nity like kings. Perhaps the smaller fish are in awe of them
and treat them with deference.

Some say that the big chaps occasionally turn cannibal,
eating their smaller brethren. An 8 lb. carp has been
caught on the small silver spoon of a pike spinner and it is
hard to see how this came about if they do not occasionally
devour one of their own kind.

There will be times—there are certain carp waters—
when all your wiles and all your endeavours will prove
unavailing. I know two localities, one in Shropshire and
one in Devon, where this is the case. The Shropshire
locality is a deep dark pool called the Church Pool. It is
surrounded by trees and looks an ideal carping place.
And so it is in so far that immense carp dwell there, but
nobody can ever catch them. Worms, paste, wasp grub,
early and late fishing—all prove wasted endeavour, and
those bronze giants continue to bask in the sun, the
despair of all anglers who, seeing them, are almost driven
to madness.

The other locality is not far from Beechmere, and is,
curiously enough, another flooded mine but very much
smaller. Many years ago a number of Beechmere carp
were transferred to this old working which, though small,
is very deep. That was fifty years ago or more. The carp
are still there, visible on hot days, but no man has ever
been known to catch them.

Whilst I write of the last locality it has brought to my
mind another, in Leicestershire.

This is a very beautiful pool close to the railway, surrounded by trees and bushes and in places very deep. It
was the place where the ballast was dug for the railway
when it was built, and it holds some very big carp indeed.

139

There are lilies in the water and altogether it is an ideal spot. But those carp are not to be caught! In the pond are good bream—good sport is had with them—but I have only met one man who has ever hooked a carp in the ballast hole and he hooked it in June on maggot.

He played it for some time, long enough for him to see it was a carp, and then he was broken.

Another man, a platelayer, who frequently poaches this pool in the early mornings, told me that one July dawn he had a tremendous run near a lily bed from something which went away like a runaway train. He never saw the fish—it speedily smashed him up—but I have no doubt it was one of the big carp.

In this water the 'sucking' sound, mentioned earlier, is very noticeable. Small carp are there in abundance as well as the big ones, but not one single small carp has, as far as I can discover, ever been caught in the Ballast Hole.

I cannot pretend to explain this phenomenon, all I can surmise is that the carp have one particular wild food they find in the pond and they prefer that to all others.

That wild food may be the transparent grubs under the lily leaves, in which case the angler is set an insurmountable problem.

This brings me to the practice of fishing for carp with maggot or paste over the edge of the lily leaves. Every carp fisher, or angler for other fish, will have read about this dodge. But I say at once, such methods are sometimes successful with small carp, and you may even conceivably deceive a big fish, but you will never land it. He will go straight into the forest of the lily roots and once there—well—there's no more to be said.

Chapter XVIII

EXPERIENCES AT WOODWATER POOL

ONE spring in the late nineteen thirties I had a letter from a man who lived on the Shropshire and Worcestershire border telling me of a wonderful pool on his estate with the promising name of Woodwater Pool. It was, he said, very deep, some four or five acres in extent, and was buried among thick woods. Like Beechmere it had at some earlier period been a mine, though its history and purpose had long been lost and not even the oldest 'local' could give information concerning it.

It had also been, at one time, a strictly preserved duck shoot, but the present owner, having no incentive for wildfowling, had little interest in it though it was still strictly preserved and nobody was allowed to angle there. His keeper, he said, could put me up if I did not mind rather cramped quarters and the keeper's house was not more than half a mile from Woodwater Pool. Knowing my interest in carp, he said that this pool contained some enormous fish, twenty pounds and over, and there were no other species in the lake save rudd. If I wished, he said, I could come as soon as the season opened, which was in June, and had he not been going away from his home he would have been only too pleased to put me up at the Hall. He was a rich bachelor and apparently every summer left that part of the country to stay on a small estate in the north of Scotland (he was a keen salmon fisher), and did not return until after the end of October when the stalking finished. This kind letter from a stranger who only knew me from my books was similar to others I have had from time to time from generous-minded sportsmen. (I had one recently from another unknown friend who offered me three thousand acres of first class rough shooting on the Pembrokeshire coast, an offer which, needless to say, I intend accepting as soon as the opportunity occurs.)

I had already made arrangements to go to Beechmere for the last two weeks of June, so I wrote and asked him if July would be convenient. I had a satisfactory reply telling me he had informed his keeper, Roscommon, I was coming and that all would be ready for me whenever I liked to go. 'I can't tell you much about the Woodwater carp,' he concluded in his letter, 'but Roscommon knows more than I do about them, as I believe he sometimes fishes for them himself. I have, however, seen them in the pool on many occasions, when I have been shooting squirrels in the woods about, and they are certainly worthy quarry and seemed to me to be astonishingly large for coarse fish, but then I know very little about coarse fishing. I hope you have some luck and I'm sure Mrs. Roscommon will make you confortable though you will no doubt find the quarters rather cramped. If you like rabbit shooting, take a gun with you or borrow Roscommon's.'

The second of July found me on my way to Wood-water by car, going by way of Rugby and Worcester, the back seat burdened with my seat basket and tackle, and hope high in my heart.

As I have just said, July is the habitual carp fisher's month, the fever is then at its height, and as I drove along the leafy lanes I formed a mental picture of what Wood-water was like. (As is always the case, it proved to be quite different from the actual place.)

It was a hot and lifeless sort of day and a few miles from Worcester I ran into a heavy thunderstorm which only aggravated my condition—thunder being the best possible tonic to wake the carp up.

I found the park and mansion with some difficulty, as it lay off the main road, buried among woods. I enquired at the lodge gates where the keeper's house was and discovered it lay across the park among the oak woods which I could see on my left. My kind host had told me I could garage the car at the Hall, so I fixed this business with the groom I found in the spacious stable yard and, with this man to help me carry my paraphernalia, I tramped across the park to the keeper's house. It was a typical dwelling of its type, very neat and quite roomy, set away among the trees which gave a fine view of the park and distant mansion. (The latter, by the way, was a pseudo-Gothic structure and not particularly beautiful, as my host, if he should read these lines, would be the first to admit.)

Our advent was heralded by vociferous barking and two fine retrievers rushed out, a black one and a yellow, which were soon called to order by Roscommon himself who quickly appeared upon the scene.

He was a man of under middle height but very powerfully built, as powerful as an ape, the shoulders broad,

143

the arms long. He was clean shaven with a red face, and the hard blue distrustful eyes of the typical gamekeeper. But he was most kind and obliging and soon I was ensconced in my ideal quarters—a sitting room to myself and several interesting examples of stuffed birds and animals, including a white badger and very fine night heron, most beautifully mounted by a well-known firm of taxidermists. Usually these unhappy birds, slain by the 'lout with the gun', are posed in ridiculous attitudes quite foreign to them. But this specimen had been set up with wonderful skill, head down and shoulders hunched, its long slender feet cautiously feeling their way among the reeds. The background too was splendidly executed and I was lost in admiration.

The history of this bird merits description. One bitter and snowy winter's night Roscommon was shooting pigeons and carrion crows in the woods near the Woodwater Pool. It was at the end of a bitter spell of weather when the lakes and streams were frozen. He made a record bag of pigeons, over sixty birds he told me, and when it became almost dark he set to work on the carrions which were coming in to roost.

As he stole among the trees he spied a dim blob far up in an oak which seemed to him to be two carrions roosting side by side. He fired and down fell a large object. He sent his retriever for it, but the dog came back with its tail between its legs. Mystified, Roscommon went to investigate and found he had slain a beautiful night heron. This poor bird, a wanderer in the snow, had no doubt been spending that bitter period of weather on Woodwater Pool and had come into the woods to sleep.

This tragic accident Roscommon, honest fellow that he was, reported at once to the 'boss', who had the bird

144

set up. That is the story of how the bird came to the cottage.

The other most interesting example of the taxidermist's art was a little bustard which had been shot on the Lincolnshire Wolds by the 'boss's' father, in the middle of the nineteenth century. Not so well mounted as the night heron, it nevertheless interested me a good deal.

I suppose I could devote a whole chapter to the keeper and his wife, to their life history and all the wonderful tales of the things he had seen in the woods, but the reader will be becoming impatient.

It can be imagined I lost no time in finding my way to the Woodwater Pool and after an excellent tea, which consisted of two duck eggs, fresh lettuce and radishes, home-made jam and other delicacies beautifully served, I accompanied the keeper and his dogs through the woods to the pool.

It was much more open than Beechmere, though surrounded on all sides by oak woods. On one side there was an ominous bluff crowned, of course, with trees, the rocks coming down, as they do at Beechmere, sheer into the dark water, which was of great depth, though Roscommon assured me it was nowhere near the depth of Beechmere, being no more than thirty feet or so at the deepest part.

And unlike Beechmere, it had great beds of lilies, some the common yellow, others white.

The western end was shallow for a considerable way and here the stream that fed the water wound away through the leafy woods, a black and sluggish stream.

That first glimpse of Woodwater was very impressive. I saw at once it looked a likely place for big carp and from what Roscommon told me, it was a virtually virgin water. He had fished it himself a little when he was young, but had no patience for the game. His son, however, also a keeper at another estate (in Shropshire) had caught some very good fish there in the 15 lb. class, though these, Roscommon assured me, were small compared with some he had seen in Woodwater.

I did not fish that first night but contented myself with baiting up a spot which took my fancy, a fine wide open space, almost square, at the south end flanked on all sides by lilies. The nearest bed was quite eighty yards distant and I thought that should I hook a fish, I should have a good chance of tiring him before he reached their sanctuary.

If one can master a large carp at his first intense rush, the battle is partly won. If you can get him moving round in circles opposite you, in deep snagless water, he should be yours if you exercise care.

I saw no fish moving that night, though it was ideal, warm and still, and I did not expect to do any good for a day or so, before the carp had found my ground bait (bread and grain). Roscommon procured for me some small potatoes that night and dug me some worms, and when I mentioned wasp grubs, he told me he could obtain me some as he knew of a nest not far from his cottage. I was determined to try all available baits. Roscommon's son had caught his fifteen pounder on bread paste, so I thought I should stand the best chance with this, but I wanted to be prepared.

Having done much useful preliminary work I had a good night's rest, being lulled to sleep by the mournful hootings of innumerable owls which called to one another in the woods about the cottage.

The still hot weather which heralded my visit to Woodwater seemed to be settled. The keeper, looking at the sky next morning, prophesied that it would continue so for several days and the weather forecast on the wireless was hopeful also.

The following evening after my arrival I ground baited my selected pitch once again, though I did not fish it.

I forgot to mention that there was, at that point, a wealth of brushwood birch on a promontory of land which extended a little way into the pool, almost an island. This place was really a 'duck butt' built by the former owner of Woodwater but had not been used for some years. It made, however, an excellent blind for a carp angler, a use to which it had never been put, and the carp would not regard it with any suspicion, as it had been there for so long.

In the middle of the lake was a small island, some un-worked portion of the mine and no doubt part of the original surface. This was thickly grown with bushes, privet and some yew and once there had been a tree there, but it had been cut down as the island was another 'duck butt' and no doubt the spreading branches made shooting difficult, indeed it is very hard to shoot birds through overhanging branches.

The island also served as a refuge to the duck from foxes and they bred there also.

Roscommon told me that, if you wish wild duck to frequent your pools, they must have an island where they can feel secure. Foxes are their great enemy, winding them and stealing on them in the dark, and ducks—mallard at least—cannot see much better in the dark than a human being, at least that is my experience.

But to return to the carp. Though I did not fish my baited spot, I kept a sharp lookout for feeding fish and

147

also put a line in at the other end of the pool, though not with much hope of hooking anything worth catching.

Fish were moving that second evening and as I stayed late I heard a few 'wallopers' jump. Many duck were in evidence as night fell. I had no bites from carp but little rudd harried my paste balls, and I found that, when I drew them in, the bread had been much nibbled by the fry. Moreover these little fish constantly bumped the line below the ledger float. The midges also were a nuisance.

But it was reassuring to hear in the gloaming the sullen plunge of great carp far out among the lilies.

Roscommon suggested that I should fish from the island as well as from my chosen pitch, and though I considered that rowing out to the place might disturb the fish, he assured me that he had frequently rowed about the pool and could glide along within a few feet of basking carp and they took no notice of him.

I therefore ground baited a second pitch on the south side of the island. It was a weedy bushy place and I had to trample down the rank growth and cut away some of the yew so that I could handle my rod.

The water was about eight feet deep ten yards out and then the bottom went suddenly down where there must have been a gallery, such as there was in Beechmere. It puzzled me why this island (it was about a quarter of an acre in extent) should have been left in the working. There was a wide sort of causeway under the water behind the island joining it to the bank where the depth was not more than four feet deep and here lilies grew in a dense mat.

If I hooked a big fish he would no doubt take me right round the island into the weeds or else make a clear straight out into the pool to another vast lily bed fifty yards away.

148

On the whole I favoured my first selection, but I resolved to give the island a fair trial, fishing it in the early morning and the 'duck butt' pitch in the evening.

During the middle of the second day (I had had no bites early and was beginning to think I should have to change my bait) Roscommon rowed me all round the lake along the fringes of the lilies and I saw one or two very big fish which were in the 15 lb. category but nothing larger.

When the sun was full out I could see, with the glasses, three enormous carp sunning off the island which were certainly over the 20 lb. mark and looked to me over thirty, but it is hard to judge the weight of fish under the surface.

That evening, fishing from the 'duck butt', I had the first run from a carp. He did not bite like a Beechmere fish, he dipped the float a very little way and left it motionless for nearly five minutes.

Then very gently he slid away with it and I struck.

A lively battle ensued and Roscommon happening along just then, he landed it for me, a carp of 7 lb. or a little under. A nice fish and a most promising beginning.

The next morning, a misty breathless dawn with a scum on the water, I rowed across to the island. I nearly fell in when disembarking from the boat, which was rather cranky, and only saved myself by catching hold of a yew bough. I then trod on a wasp's nest and it might have been awkward on that confined place, but the wasps 'lost' me when I pushed through the bushes.

I had made a certain amount of noise getting out to the island and I thought that I had scared every fish within yards of me. When I settled down to fish I saw bubbles come up which looked promising.

My float had been in position for about an hour and the sun was just coming up over the oak woods when the quill registered the first bite. I have a note of it in my journal—the time was exactly 7.15 a.m., rather late for a July carp to bite.

This bite was exactly similar to the one I had the previous night, though before going gently away he laid the float flat on the water like a bream.

I knew at once when I struck I was into no specimen fish though he fought well enough—a carp of 4½ lbs. I had another similar fish about half an hour afterwards in exactly the same place. That evening (July 4th) fishing from the 'duck butt' I had one bite, very late, which I unaccountably missed. I still 'fancied' the 'duck butt' pitch, somehow I had no faith that a big carp would be caught from the island.

Next morning, another misty morning, after an intensely hot night (which in my case was full of amazing dreams about carp packed so tightly in a pool that one could walk over them!) I was again at the island, this time an hour earlier, about a quarter to six. I sat for two hours watching my motionless float and listening to the wood pigeons cooing in the woods all around, a beautiful concert of sound. I also note that I saw an otter come half out of the water opposite the island where it rested its forepads on a sunken log. It then dived and I did not see it again.

This made me think that further fishing was useless, as when there is an otter in a pond the carp usually are aware of the fact and can telegraph the news.

But five minutes after I had seen the otter I had a run. The fish took me straight away, slowly, with the float still at half cock. The white quill glided with ever-increasing

150

momentum and then stopped as though the fish had left the bait. I was leaning forward with my hand on the butt feeling the hammering of my heart (absurd as it may seem I get childishly excited when big carp are about) and the next moment the reel simply screamed.

He made straight round the island, narrowly missing some overhanging yew branches, which I made a mental note to speak to Roscommon about later, and then, just when I thought he was into the lilies he turned and made out into the centre of the pool in one spectacular power dive.

I think he went very deep for he churned the water up a good deal and then there was a 'heavy boil'. I should say he took out about thirty or forty yards of line. The next half hour was a slow procession round and round, to and fro, in front of the island. Up to now I had not caught a single glimpse of my adversary so could form no idea of his size, but I knew him to be very large.

At last I caught my first and last view of him, easily the largest carp I have ever had on my tackle and very close to the twenty pound mark, possibly over. He came in sideways, looking very tired, I could see the bold criss-cross 'wire netting' pattern of his scales (he was a common carp), and I think what impressed me most was not his length, which was possibly some three feet or so, but his depth, he was a prodigious bronze *tub* of a fish. Then he gave one thrust of his pectorals and went straight down.

I felt fairly confident I was going to land him and looked round for my net and with a very horrid pang indeed remembered I had left it in the boat—I am unfortunately an absent-minded fellow.

Now to reach the boat I had to push through the bushes for a distance of some thirty yards and this necessitated leaving the rod to look after the carp. It was impossible to walk to the place holding the rod, as the yews were too thick and high.

Feeling the fish was fairly sluggish and tired, I put the rod gently down with the butt in the rod rest to leave the reel free and made a wild dash through the bushes to the boat which I had moored to a sapling. Grabbing the net I plunged madly back and as I did so heard the wicked tearing screech of my reel again. The carp, after a rest, had evidently made up his mind to make a last bid for freedom.

This bid was successful for, just as I reached the rod, gasping and panting, there was a terrific boil among the lilies opposite and the line came slack.

When I examined the cast I found it had gone where the No. 8 hook was joined to the cast—a clear break (it was before the days of alasticum wire).

I feel confident that if I had not been so foolish as to forget my net that carp would now be regarding me from a glass case and my obsession would be cured. As it was I reeled in my line sorrowfully and, packing up, went home to breakfast.

Yet, despite my disappointment, I was full of confidence. I had another ten days before me, the weather appeared to be settled, I had found the right bait and it only was a matter of time before I was into an equally good fish. But confident optimism is dangerous in the habitual carp fisher and I was to be disillusioned.

The next day the weather broke, a cold and rainy spell followed and I had no more notable fish for the rest of my stay.

The following year, when I wrote again to my unknown friend, I was grieved to learn that he had sold this estate and the incoming tenant, a keen man with a gun and breeder of duck, would allow no one to disturb the place.

So the Woodwater Pool carp are again unassailable and the chance to fish for them may not return during the remaining years that are left to me.

It is amazing how, after a lifetime in pursuit of carp, the 'addict' becomes extraordinarily sensitive to the approach of fish, how he can tell, almost from the appearance of the surface of the water when carp are 'on feed'.

I noticed this to be very marked when I was fishing a carp pool in Hertfordshire. During the day the water appears 'dead' but as soon as dusk falls and all breeze dies away one begins to look for 'signs'. On a perfectly calm pool slight undulations may be noticed. They are very insignificant but the practised eye can see them. These undulations are caused by big fish moving about *on the bottom of the pond*. When the sun shines during the day most carp will be close to the surface, swimming to and fro, sometimes in shoals, sometimes singly or in pairs. At this time they are not on feed though they may be tempted to take floating crust. I have frequently tried to catch basking carp by a crust suspended in mid-water. One small shot will keep the cast anchored on the pool bed while the air in the crust will make it rise to the limit of its 'tether'. At such times I have seen carp swim past without taking the smallest interest in the bait. It is simply that they are not hungry and that they are enjoying the warming rays on their scaly backs. Many process back and forth, I am sure, to obtain exercise, just as people walk on land.

I think that I was extremely unlucky not to catch my record carp at Woodwater; pure carelessness on my part cost me my prize.

Chapter XIX

THE LAST DAY OF THE SEASON

I HAVE just been putting away my tackle and have held in my hand a little scarlet-tipped quill which has been a faithful friend and lucky talisman for several seasons. Many times it has traversed submarine depths following its prey, like stoat pursues quarry, many times has it explored shadowed fathoms unseen by the eye of man.

It has frequently disappeared from view in the nether pit of Beechmere and has no doubt witnessed some interesting battles and doings of bulky carp. It has become enmeshed in sunken trees, and has, on many occasions, been tangled in willow branches, lily pads and weed banks. Yet somehow it returns to my basket as faithfully as a homing pigeon and will, I hope, be my cheerful companion in many another carping expedition in the years to come. Only yesterday, at fall of eve, it tracked a mailed and weighty warrior into the depths of a pool. Alas! it was not in at the death, for death there was not; that invisible muscular adversary dismembered my gear among sunken thickets and I had to reel sadly in.

154

It was the last day of the season, a day in mid-September, by which time carp are thinking of going downstairs and taking up their quarters for the winter. After weeks of hot sunlight, scorched pastures, withering trees and bushes, the rain had come. It came softly, sweetly, in the night watches, a refreshing hissing fall which has so eagerly been awaited by the parched land. At dawn, when I arose, it was still gently falling, making rings in the rockery pool. I stole about the house like a felon so as not to awaken my family; I crept in stockinged feet into the kitchen and grilled myself some kippers, and the rich aroma filled the sleeping, disregarding house.

Outside the sky was growing ever lighter. Some young swallows, perched upon my willow, roused themselves and stretched, leaning forward and raising their little wings so that the back of each touched its fellow, which is the way a bird stretches its 'arms'.

Another yawned and tucked in his head again, yet another began to twitter and preen, casting an eye towards the sky where pearl-grey rain-clouds hurried over. I felt a pang of sorrow that they would soon be gone, that I should have to wait for seven long months before I saw them again.

My breakfast done and tackle packed I was away, calling for a friend nine miles distant and going on from there to this unknown pool. Unknown carp pools are always a delight, and this proved to be no exception.

It lay among remote Leicestershire pastures, visible only when you had penetrated a veil of thick trees. Standing in the nearby lane you would not have guessed a pool was there. The way in, through some double gates, was locked and barred, and the confines of the wood hedged about with many strands of barbed wire. I have yet to

155

meet the barbed wire which can keep *me* out and, having a clear conscience as the permit was in my friend's pocket, we wriggled through a rabbit run with the agility and expedition of small unbreeched urchins.

First there was an awful pond, set in a hole, black as the nether pit and upon whose ebony face rotifers gyrated. Heaven knows what depth it was; to me it appeared fathomless! On one side was a cloudy weed cushion, deep under the surface, a fungoid-looking growth with scarlet tentacles, on the other an ashen blasted tree whose writhing naked branches were reflected in the inky waters.

But what a pond for carp! and how impossible it would be to ever get one out! This was not the water where we were to fish however—that lay a hundred yards on and was a much less forbidding place. To reach it we threaded a pleasant wild woodland where blackthorn and teazel flourished and jays scolded. And then, in a step or two, a vista opened both charming and rare, the sight of an irregular pool of about an acre in extent, its banks bushed with thick trees—sycamore, ash, oak. The rain in the night had moistened the leaves which had fallen about their feet, leaves decayed before their time owing to the dry hot summer. From this fallen damp carpet which rustled under our feet there arose the most exquisite perfume which took me back immediately to the days of my babyhood. Each day in the winter our governess, a dear little lady called Miss Nicholson (who is still living, I am glad to say), took us down to the post office in the village about a quarter of a mile from our house. The road at that spot was overhung with elms, limes, and some sycamores, and was never dry from September to May.

Of course, in those days, there was no tarmac, and I

156

well remember the ridges of soft mud left by the pram wheels as we went along. From this moist muddy road where fallen leaves were ground into the mud to form a sort of porridge there used to arise this same smell which I noticed and recognised yesterday.

While we were setting up our rods on a little promontory, whose worn, cracked earth suggested it was a much frequented angling post, an enormous butterfly swooped over the trees and flapped over the water, dipping once into it before soaring over the opposite wood. What it was I had no idea and have never seen any British insect like it.

The water was not very clear and was of considerable depth, close to the bank it was eight feet or so and a much greater depth in the centre. I cannot say that the pool appeared to me exactly 'carpy', it was perhaps too cheerful and tended a spot; the fishermen's seats, hut, and neat paths may have given this impression. However that may be, I had no run on stout ledger tackle and it was not until after lunch, when I was walking round the pond on the wood side, that I saw any sign of carp. Then I spied a common carp of about three pounds swimming in a deep bay half screened by willows. A little farther on a fat mirror, he looked 2 lbs. and had a most benevolent face, was lazily swimming close to the bank. I noticed him rise now and again to have a look at small floating willow leaves, one of which he actually took into his mouth and swam down with it, expelling it when he had swum a dozen yards or more.

I thought I might have a chance at him with floating bread, and though he did not appear more than 2 lbs. I took off my ledger and substituted a lighter greased line and roach hook to gut which I tied direct to the line.

The cherub-like mirror disappeared, but about ten minutes later I observed his bluish form swimming below the crust. He did not seem to see it at first. He then came and had a close inspection of a willow leaf two yards from my bait (which by then must have been fairly sodden as it had been immersed for quite a quarter of an hour or more).

He then noticed the bread. He swam round it twice, came close, stared at it, turned away, and came upwind, just as Burton says they do. It was my first experience of this method in open water and the thrill was great even though it was no record fish. He sucked it in, turned swiftly about, and the line slipped through the rings. I never struck him, just tightened, and for ten minutes we had a pretty exhibition. I saw he was bigger than I thought at first and when at last my friend slipped the net under him as I towed him past, head out of water, he was soon kicking in the folds. A second later he was flopping on the grass, a fish of 4 lbs. exactly, by my pocket scales.

This shows how deceptive it is to judge carp in the water. I should never have guessed it *was* a four pounder. It made me think of a Bedfordshire pool and a huge balloon-like form of a big chap I once saw one summer day. That fish must have been nearer thirty than twenty if this 'mirror' was anything to go by!

When the carp had been returned to the pool the sun went in and I changed to worm, a lob, fished on the same tackle but with my favourite scarlet-tipped quill before mentioned. About an hour later, just before sundown, the scarlet tip sank from sight and a terrific 'pull' ripped off the reel line as the fish made straight across the pond. Against the far bank was a sunken briar bush and into this my carp went—and that was that. I had no 'banjo string' to hold him off and a break was inevitable.

What this fish weighed I have no ideas as, of course, I never saw it but I am sure it was a common carp from the power of his first rush, mirrors never seem to possess such strength.

As we had used up the last of the 'lobs' and a mournful autumnal wind began to rustle in the trees, we packed up our tackle and came away, threading the winding paths among the thickets where already leaves of sloe were turning salmon pink.

Such was the last day of the season, a sorrowful occasion but one on which I look back with considerable pleasure.

After September is out most carp go below and stay there until the following spring. I do not think this pretty pool contains any record breakers, indeed I am not sure many carp are there; they certainly do not breed as there is not enough weed. I also had the impression it was overstocked. Roach, perch and pike are never the best bedfellows to carp.

The chief interest for me in yesterday's expedition was the opportunity to try the floating bread method in open water. Without a wind it is difficult to get the crust out. I was fortunate in having a backing breeze from exactly the right quarter, indeed I once floated the crust right across the pool, paying out the line as the wind took the bait. I also experimented with a small raft made from a scrap of bark, resting the bread upon it.

But with the 'boat' method I usually manage to get some tangles in my coiled line; a single blade of grass, a leaf or twig, will cause the moving line to 'snarl', the bait is jerked off the 'boat' and the whole laborious business has to be begun again.

159

It is an exciting business to see a great fish turn into the wind, grab your bread crust in one sullen salmon-like lunge, and make off with it.

As to river fishing, I have never fished for carp in rivers though I have seen one or two very fine specimens, one notable fish from the Nene near Billing Mill is in the Natural History Museum in Northampton. Near that town there are some flooded pits which have the reputation of holding specimen fish, and anglers occasionally capture one on floating bread but so far I have been unsuccessful.

Sound tackle is essential when going 'all out' for big carp; it must be of the very best. Your line, casts, hooks and reels must be looked over as carefully as the salmon fisher checks up on his gear.

I have little to add to these notes, I have told all I know about big carp. I feel that I have no authority to write a book on carp fishing as I have never caught a very big one—a ten pounder is my best. But the reader will, perhaps, have guessed this. It may well be that even now, at this very hour, there is, somewhere in some county, a tough old alderman which is destined to fulfil my lifelong ambition. There he swims in that unknown water, questing perhaps, like a great bronze hog among the dark forest of the lily roots. Our destinies may be united, and my desires will be satisfied! But now the red leaves of autumn whirl, the wind pipes mournfully among the trees, leaden ripples lap on lonely forgotten shores.

I think this autumn night of Beechmere, wrapped in deepest shadow, the beechen tops restless and hissing in the wind, the sinister dark waters brooding and waiting, barely ruffled by an occasional puff of air.

I think of my other well-loved haunts wrapped in the
160

mantle of this same night with the owls calling among the woods and foxes setting out for their evening's hunting.

I think of Woodwater, of how the stars are now shining down on its broad fine acres, whilst high overhead fly the migrating birds.

I heard only the other day that, during the war, a German plane dropped an oil bomb one night into Woodwater, no doubt mistaking the pale glimmering expanse for some cringing town. But I doubt whether the carp suffered much harm.

My rods are laid up in their cases, my tackle put away, the summer has gone.

But summer days will come again, and yet again, and if I am spared I will be there once more, beside the pools I know and love, listening to the cooing of wood pigeons yet unborn, smelling the wild sweet water as it smokes in the summer dawn.

Being an habitual carp fisher, I am content to wait. After all, waiting is part of the game, I am well used to it.

Chapter XX

THE KING OF CARP

To conclude this book I give two most interesting extracts from a fishing book by Wilhelm Kovacshazy entitled *Horgaszbottal* sent to me by Mr. L. P. Davis of the Information Services Branch, C.M.F. Mr. Davis had read my *Fisherman's Bedside Book* and was so impressed by the accounts of battles with big carp that he thought I might care to read these extracts and possibly incorporate them in my 'Confessions' which I told him I was writing. The style is very reminiscent of Aksakov.

British anglers know little of the habits of the carp abroad and for this reason they are, I think, doubly interesting.

One of the old philosophers once remarked that fortune favoured everybody at least once in a lifetime, but that most people failed to recognise the right moment: he who

162

ignored the fickle goddess would never be allowed to grasp the chance again.

Such moments tend to occur more than once in the life of an angler or hunter. Let me relate a case that happened to me.

Soon after the 1914-18 war a friend of mine, also a passionate angler, invited me to spend my holidays with him in a village on the shores of Lake Balaton, where we would fish for *fogosh* (the famous pike-perch of Lake Balaton). At that time the fishing possibilities of this vast expanse of water were practically undiscovered by sportsmen, and for a number of years we were undisputed masters of the fishing grounds. Things have changed since then, but we still treasure grateful memories of ten perfect fishing holidays spent there.

By chance I was introduced one day to the art of fishing for carp. We had made an excursion to Keszthely and, on the way back, met an old acquaintance on the train. Noticing my fishing gear he enquired how many carp I had caught.

'We don't fish for carp,' I replied, 'we only catch *fogosh*.'

'And how big are they?'

'Oh, not very big, about 4 to 8 ounces.'

'Isn't it rather boring catching such small fry?' my friend asked.

'Why, do you by any chance catch sharks?'

'Well, not exactly. But in the space of two weeks I have caught seventeen carp. None of them weighed less than four pounds, and my bag included two of twelve pounds and one eighteen pounder. I have also hooked some even heavier fish, which I lost again. On the day of my departure I went down to a spot by the edge of the reeds where

I had been ground-baiting, and a whale of a carp took my bait. Try as I would, I couldn't tire him. He fought so powerfully and with such determination that he broke my rod and my very strong line and escaped. And that is the third time this has happened to me!'

My friend's tale of the great carp excited my angler's imagination. Perhaps I would never have started to fish for carp, had I not been told of the existence of such rod-destroying, line-breaking, ferocious fish. It would be worth one's while to pit one's wits against a fellow like that!

I took the first opportunity of buying hooks and a line suitable for carp and returned to Balatongyörök, the village on Lake Balaton.

'From now on I am going to fish for carp,' I told my friend John.

He smiled: 'You are, are you? Better have a talk with Michael Varga, the professional fisherman. He knows the lake like his pocket and is sure to show you a spot where there are carp.'

However, I did not ask Michael, much as I regretted this later on. For a whole week I sought the carp in vain. I did manage to catch four, but none of them scaled more than two pounds.

Rowing back to the boathouse one morning, who should help me out of the boat but Michael Varga? Glancing at my meagre catch he shook his head and said: 'You're fishing at a hopeless spot, sir. The water is too shallow next to the reeds there, and the bottom far too muddy. You'll rarely find a large carp stray to a spot like that.'

'Where would I stand a better chance?' I asked.

'I'm free this afternoon,' Michael volunteered. 'If you

like, we'll look for a better spot and also have a look at the old one.'

The sun was very hot that afternoon and no breath of air disturbed the smooth mirror-like surface of the lake. As arranged, Michael appeared at the boathouse at half past two, carrying with him a reedcutter with a long handle.

We got into the boat and Michael took hold of the oars. With quiet, sure strokes he headed out for the reedbeds.

Arriving there, he dipped the oars into the water carefully, avoiding any splashing and rowing very slowly. Keeping a steady distance of eight to ten yards from the edge of the reeds, he silently pointed to a number of different places. In vain did I strain my eyes, I saw nothing. Later on, I at least noticed a slight movement or an almost imperceptible rustling noise among the reeds, whenever the oars slightly stirred the water—although Michael dipped them into it almost noiselessly—and the carp, noticing the approach of something strange, fled into the reedbeds.

Michael let the boat drift and instructed me: 'Look carefully in the direction I am pointing out, sir. There in the shady part of the reeds, near the open water, some eight or ten inches below the surface, you will see the carp; there are many of them enjoying the sun to-day.'

I tried to follow Michael's instructions. For quite a while I saw nothing. Then, gradually, as if my eyes had been enchanted, I began to perceive large, motionless fishes, hugging the edge of the reedbed no more than a couple of hands below the surface.

We continued to row along the edge of the reeds, which stretch as far as Keszthely. I noticed innumerable carp, from four and five up to sixteen and even twenty pounds.

Hardly stirring a fin, they seemed to be asleep in the sun. No sooner, however, did the boat get closer to them, when they suddenly allowed themselves to sink into the depths or fled into the rustling reeds. Finally my eyes became so experienced that I even noticed that the larger specimens were the more careful ones and that they dived or fled earlier than their smaller brethren.

In the meantime we had reached my old pitch. Michael thrust one of the oars into the water: the depth hardly exceeded one yard, but it was no difficult matter to press the oar into the mud for another yard and a half. On lifting the oar back into the boat, we saw that the blade was coated with grey, slimy mud.

'This is a bad spot,' said Michael, 'the mud is too deep and the water too shallow. Carp don't like that. I could find you a better place near here, but I'd like to suggest that we row over to the stretch of water near the houses, where the bottom near the high reeds is clear and the water deep. You'll be sure to find large carp there.'

'All right,' I consented, 'let's try it there.'

After some twenty minutes of rowing, Michael arrived at the chosen spot.

Here the reedbeds extended some sixty or seventy yards from the shores of the lake and were so thick that it would hardly have been possible to penetrate through them with a boat. Small bays cut into them and here the growth was not quite so thick.

Michael stopped the boat in one of these bays and, keeping close to the reeds, tried to measure the depth with the aid of an oar. Although this was nearly three yards long, he failed to reach the bottom.

He was satisfied. 'The water is deep here,' he said, 'and the bottom consists of good, hard clay. There is a thin layer of mud as far as the reeds and after that the clay bottom stretches far into the lake. Carp love to rest in this deep water. Then, when they start to move, they swim up to the reeds and forage for food. This will be a grand pitch for you, sir.'

Michael then began to prepare the pitch for me. First he removed all odd reed stalks which might have got into the way of my line. After that he rowed right up to the edge of the reedbed and, taking hold of some thirty stalks, tied them into a big bunch with the aid of some wire. This process was repeated some four yards further along, and lo and behold! I had a first rate anchorage.

'Those reed bundles will hold the boat even in rough weather,' he assured me.

I thoroughly liked the look of the place. By good fortune—or maybe by the foresight of Michael—it even faced north, so that the sun did not hurt my eyes.

The next step was to bait up the place. I used nearly four pounds of maize, cooked to a nicety, and distributed it along the edge of the reedbed. This I repeated on the following three days.

On the fourth morning, at 6 a.m., I rowed out for the first time with the intention of fishing.

Stealthily I approached my pitch and was most careful to avoid making the slightest sound with my oars. I was practically holding my breath whilst I baited my hook with maize prior to casting out to the edge of the reedbed on my left.

Hardly a few minutes had passed, when the float suddenly began to move and then disappeared altogether. I struck and the line tightened. The fish was putting up a good fight and felt heavy, but after a few moments the line slackened and came back to me. I had struck too early and the fish had managed to free itself.

On the following day I was more successful. I caught three carp, but their total weight was no more than ten pounds.

With that I had broken the ice. Soon I had caught a mirror carp of eight pounds and a 'wild' carp of eleven pounds. The latter gave me such a tug when I struck him that I nearly fell out of the boat. He fought so fiercely and so tenaciously that I was inclined to mistrust my scales when they showed no more than eleven pounds.

These wild carp,[1] recognisable by the elongated body and the small scales covering the whole of it, generally fight so fiercely that only in the rarest cases is a really big one caught. Usually something breaks or the hook is torn free.

One morning early a mist covered Lake Balaton. The sky was grey and hardly a sunbeam penetrated the thick layers of clouds. Noiselessly I approached my usual place and cast out my line. No sooner had the float cocked itself, when it began to give unmistakable signs of the bait having aroused the interest of a fish. Taking up the rod, I prepared to strike but by that time the float once more lay motionless. The fish had removed the bait without touching the hook. I baited up again and made another cast. The bait could have hardly reached the bottom, when my float suddenly disappeared in a most determined manner. I struck at once.

But what has happened? Have I hooked a rock?

My line is tight and it seems as if I have caught the bottom of the lake. Whatever it is, I can't move it, though I try hard enough. Finally the strain eases a little and I am

[1] Our 'common' carp in England—Ed.

able to regain some line. The fish shows less resistance and allows me to drag him nearer to the boat.

Staring into the slightly coloured water I reel in and . . . get the fright of my life.

A huge, uncouth apparition slowly surfaces no more than a couple of yards from the boat. The pale mouth gapes, it must be ten inches in diameter. The line disappears in his gullet, only the shaft of the hook is visible somewhere in the depths. The water rushes through the open gills and the pectoral fins move slowly and evenly not unlike a ship's screw. The gleaming scales are the size of silver dollars and the dorsal fin reminds me of a sail. Indeed, a huge, a powerful carp!

Now he has seen me! He makes a sudden flight towards the reeds, but I am prepared.

Suddenly lifting the tip of my rod, I succeed in getting his head up, and, carried forward by his own impetus, he gains the open water.

I breathe again, but I know that my troubles are by no means over yet.

Twenty-five yards are between us now, and it is time to turn him again. Once more I lift the rod, begin to reel in and to slowly lead the fish back to the boat.

Thank heavens that worked! Now I shall have to reel in faster and take care to ensure that the line remains tight, because I know there will be another flight as soon as he feels the slightest loosening.

And now I can also take a side view of my monstrous antagonist. His length is at least four feet and a half!

Once more he begins to work away from me and I can hardly keep him out of the reeds. I feel the cold sweat breaking on my forehead.

Again I prevent him from gaining safety in the reeds.

169

His flight takes him out into the open water; will I be able to land him after all?

He seems to be less sure of himself now, his flights are irregular and he is continuously changing direction. I apply more strain and he shakes his head. Obviously he is beginning to feel vexed.

Now he makes what appears to be a supreme effort. Impetuously he charges into the open water.

I have a notion that something will go wrong, my rod is bent to its utmost and the line sings like a harp-string.

My heart is beating like mad, my throat is parched and I can hardly breathe.

Now I must try and turn him, my reel is nearly empty. He is still tearing away powerfully, fighting for his life and for his freedom. He wallows in the water, jumps, and again pulls with all his might.

All attempts to get some line back on the reel are in vain. I even climb into the bow of the boat in order to regain a yard or two. All to no avail. I can't move him an inch. The fish is fighting furiously, churning up the water. Suddenly the line snaps and I stumble back, nearly falling over the seat.

The line is slack and from the end a length is missing. With it the lead, the trace, the hook and my monster carp. . . .

Discouraged and exhausted I untied the boat, and, knees still atremble, I rowed home.

My lunch was waiting by the time I returned, but I could hardly eat a bite and was seriously thinking of giving up fishing on Lake Balaton and of departing the following day.

That afternoon a thunderstorm broke at about four p.m. and from then till six o'clock it rained continuously.

Fishing was out of the question for my friends as well, and, as was usual in such circumstances, we met in the inn. I told them my tale of woe, without, however, arousing much sympathy. On the contrary, they pulled my leg and only John tried to console me. 'Never mind,' he said, 'you'll get many a big 'un yet!'

Their attitude had embittered me even more, and I soon dropped the subject.

I went home, had supper, and went for a walk, ending up near the boathouse, where I sat down and gazed across the lake.

It was a clear, calm night, the moon was nearly full and the air sweet and mild after the rain. I smoked one cigarette after the other as I once more lived through the morning's fight, my nerves still on edge and my eyes unable to forget the sight of that majestic carp.

'Good evening, sir.' Michael's well-known voice suddenly reached me through the darkness.

'Good evening, Michael! Come closer and sit down. I'd like to tell you something.'

Michael joined me and I related the whole story of my adventure in all details: when and how I had hooked the fish, his flights and how I had parried them, how he had finally broken loose, and how vexed I was with myself to have lost him in the end.

'Didn't you see five gleaming, white protuberances on the shoulders of the fish, like a five-pointed crown?' Michael asked, and, thinking back, it really seemed to me as if I had seen a number of protruding white spots near its head.

'If the fish you hooked wore this white crown, you'll never succeed in landing it. It is the biggest fish in the whole of Lake Balaton, the "King of Carp". Nobody knows how old it is, it may well be more than a hundred. Twenty-five years ago our most famous harpooneer struck him with his great, five-pronged harpoon, whilst the fish was sunning himself in deep water. Even then he was a giant, who fought back with all the power at his command. In the end he succeeded in upsetting the boat, throwing the fisherman into the water. But even then our harpooner held on to his weapon, the fight continued in the water until finally the flesh of the carp gave way, the fish escaped. The fisherman, half drowned, was saved by his friends, and the carp, too, recovered in spite of his wounds. Flesh grew where the prongs of the harpoon had bitten into his body and now it looks as if the fish is wearing a five-pointed crown. He is nearly twice as big as the second largest fish of the lake, and perhaps this is the first time in his life that he has felt a hook. He has often been caught in nets, but each time he has made good his escape, generally by tearing the net to pieces. The fishermen of Lake Balaton know him well and fear him, for they know he will tear their nets to shreds. So don't feel grieved, sir, that you lost him, be grateful that he didn't drag you into the water.'

I gave some thought to what Michael had told me. Many tales of this kind have been born on the shores of Lake Balaton, but there is always a grain of truth at the bottom of them. And so there was in Michael's tale. Don't we anglers forever wait for the monster fish, the king of fish, to take our bait? It is he we dream of when we watch our float for hours on end, whether from the shore or from the boat. And when, finally, he does take our bait, he laughs at our dreams, gives an almighty tug and breaks us.

Michael's tale had given me back my peace of mind. It was late, and so we walked home.

172

'Nevertheless,' I said to Michael, 'I won't rest until I have caught this King of Carp!'

'You'll never catch him, sir. Many another good one, but the King, the one so many would like to catch, will always elude you!'

Early the following morning I was back on my pitch and ever since I have been waiting for the carp monarch of Lake Balaton.

Already I have caught one carp of twenty-eight pounds, many large ones, and even more smaller ones, but never again have I encountered the giant that broke me on a misty summer morning of 1924.

I have often told my friends this story, and one, a witty fellow, once replied:

'I know a similar story.'

'What would that be?'

'Josef was serving his time in Vienna, way before the war. After his return to his village, his father asked him: "Well, have you seen the old Emperor?" "Once," replied Josef, "but then it wasn't him." '

And yet, I maintain, it *was* him!

THE WEDDING OF THE CARP

Whitsunday and the beginning of June, early morning and brilliant sunshine on Lake Balaton.

The lake, not a stir on its surface, stretches for miles in its light-blue loveliness. In the direction of the poplars of Szentgyörgy a slight haze dims the outline of the shore. Further to the left, the reflection of the water gives the land an appearance of floating in mid-air.

The hills of Badacsony, Tatika, Somlo and Szigliget bathed in sunlight, complete the beautiful panorama.

Deep in thoughts I am sitting by the waterside and enjoying the indescribably peaceful scene.

Suddenly Michael, the fisherman, comes running up to me, excitement written all over his face.

'Sir, the carp are spawning!' he brings out breathlessly and points to the shallows near the edge of the lake.

We walk along the shore on the shingle. In the reedy water I can discover but a few small carp, which take fright on our approach and flee into the open water.

'Right now, we ought to be at the mouth of the Tapolca brook, where you can see the whole of the wedding procession of the carp, which spawn further inland in the inundation area. That's something to remember!' said Michael.

Making a quick decision, I replied: 'Give me half an hour, and I'll have the motor-boat ready!'

In those days the artificial road between Tördemic, Szigliget and Ederics had not yet been built, and the many hundred acres of moorland between Tapolca and the lake, a maze of reeds, stagnant pools and odd islands of solid ground, had not yet been drained. This formed the so-called Hollow of Tapolca, and through it the Tapolca brook made its way to the lake. In those days its bed had not yet been regulated, with the result that it burst its banks regularly every spring and formed a huge lake. But no matter how dry the weather might become, some larger or smaller pools, or even deep and muddy ponds, remained for the rest of the year. In parts, especially near Szigliget, a thick crust of mire covered the area. Folklore tells of a cart drawn by oxen that had lost its way, and, intending to cross the apparently shallow water, was buried in the mire until only the horns of the oxen protruded.

This extensive hollow offered a safe and undisturbed

spawning ground to the immense stock of carp which Lake Balaton could still boast of in those days.

Since then the area has been drained. The spawning ground has been destroyed and nowadays only an occasional carp will stray into the Tapolca brook, but, not being able to find a suitable place to spawn, will soon turn back and look for another and more hospitable place.

In those days, however, under the guidance of Michael, we found there a virgin corner of this earth.

We got into the motor-boat and headed straight for Szigliget.

Brilliant sunshine accompanied us. The screw of the motor dug a deep furrow into the sheet of water.

Gliding past the reeds the boat disturbed countless carp, which took fright and fled into the protective jungle of the rushes. Michael, unable to make himself heard above the din of the engine, continuously pointed out with his hands the size of the fish.

Twenty minutes later we were approaching the shore of Szigliget and the mouth of the Tapolca brook beneath the walls of the old castle.

We were still quite a distance from the mouth of the brook when I shut off the engine and Michael took up the oars, rowing gently and hardly lifting them out of the water.

We brought the boat to a standstill to the left of the mouth of the brook and Michael made it fast by securely tying it to two sheafs of reeds. He told me not to move too much and to speak only in a subdued voice. Having thus prepared ourselves, he pointed into the depths after a few minutes.

At first I could distinguish nothing in the opalescent but nevertheless transparent water. But soon my eyes got accustomed to the reflection of the sunlight and now I could already perceive the carp in the bed of the brook making their way upstream. At short intervals tightly packed families of twenty or thirty carp passed us, keeping close to the bottom of the brook.

Nearly all the larger carp of at least four pounds were glorying in their pinkish wedding dress. Some of the even larger ones, that hadn't been touched by the flame of love, and smaller, still immature specimens put in an appearance in their workaday clothes. These had joined the procession not by reason of the urge of propagation, but out of a sociable instinct, just as the aged and the children join in a village wedding procession.

Toward mid-day the procession became even livelier. The shoals, too, increased in size.

The sight was so interesting and charming that I had no desire to take the boat upstream and watch the spawning itself. I preferred to stay where I was.

About one p.m., as far as I could observe below the surface, the carp arrived in their thousands. They passed us in hosts and throngs. Sometimes I was under the impression that I was seeing more fish than water and some shoals were packed so tightly that there would have been no room for any more carp. Fish by fish, dressed closely together, they passed us like a living chain.

Every now and then, deep at the bottom of the brook, we would notice some giant carp. Lazily, hardly moving its fins, it would follow its fellows upstream.

Through refraction everything appears to be slightly enlarged in opalescent water. For that reason it is difficult to assess the weight and size of a fish under such circumstances. I tried to estimate the weight of the larger specimens taking into account the enlarging quality of the water and the sunbeams and I saw hundreds of carp in this procession, of which every one had his good twenty pounds and more. But there were also some of more than thirty pounds.

The procession continued endlessly and without interruption. The scales in their nuptial splendour refracted the sunbeams and dipped the whole wedding procession into a sea of glittering colours of yellow, pink, brown, purple and greenish blue. It seemed as if all jewels and all the colours of the rainbow were being reflected in this mass of fishes.

Following the eternal laws of nature, the vast host of Lake Balaton carp were on their pilgrimage to the waters of the Hollow of Tapolca, where they would wed. The fate of their weak, unprotected progeny, however, they would leave in the hands of nature.

This rare and enchantingly beautiful scene captivated me. I was not able to tear myself away. I forgot my surroundings and was entranced by the gorgeous display of colours. Somehow I felt that I was privileged by being granted a momentary glimpse of the mystic powers of nature, the renewal of eternal life.

It was very hot. Not a breath of air moved and we were perspiring freely. Nevertheless we continued to watch in devout silence and with the greatest interest.

Although I gradually became hungry and thirsty I could have continued to watch the wedding procession of the carp for hours; however, we had to be on our way, as I was expecting guests.

Michael cast off and I started the engine. As soon as we reached the open water, the reed bay seemed to close up behind us and hid the mouth of the brook. Only the remaining walls of Castle Szigliget marked the spot that had afforded us so rare a pleasure.

It was already late in the afternoon by the time we returned.

Slowly I got out of the boat. But even to-day I am as impressed by the mysterious phenomenon of nature I witnessed as I was when I returned from the mouth of the Tapolca brook that afternoon.

Gratefully I shook Michael Varga's rough fisher-hand before walking back to the inn.

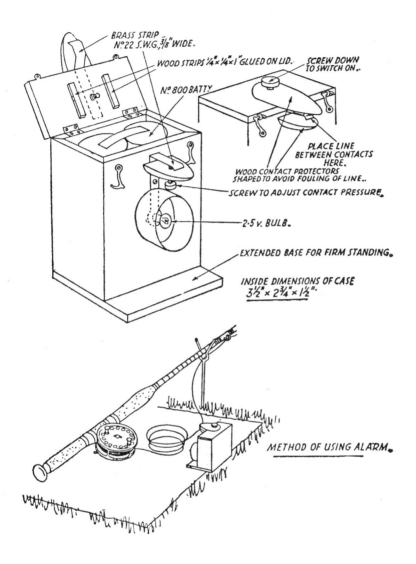

BRASS STRIP
Nº 22 S.W.G. ⅜" WIDE.

WOOD STRIPS ¼"× ¼"× I" GLUED ON LID.

SCREW DOWN
TO SWITCH ON.

Nº 800 BATTY.

PLACE LINE
BETWEEN CONTACTS
HERE.

WOOD CONTACT PROTECTORS
SHAPED TO AVOID FOULING OF LINE..

SCREW TO ADJUST CONTACT PRESSURE.

2·5 v. BULB.

EXTENDED BASE FOR FIRM STANDING.

INSIDE DIMENSIONS OF CASE
3½" × 2¾" × 1½".

METHOD OF USING ALARM.

Diagram of a nocturnal carp fisher's alarm bell, specially designed for lazy and somnolent anglers by Richard Walker.

This contrivance enables those afflicted with "Carp Fever" to gain a little sleep.